Letters, Sentences And Maxims

By
Earl Of Philip Dormer Stanhope Chesterfield

Letters, Sentences and Maxims
by Earl of Philip Dormer Stanhope Chesterfield

Copyright © 2023

ISBN: 978-93-59395-69-2

Published by

DOUBLE 9 BOOKS

2/13-B, Ansari Road, Daryaganj
New Delhi – 110002
info@double9books.com
www.double9books.com
Tel. 011-40042856

This book is under public domain

ABOUT THE AUTHOR

In the 18th century, Philip Dormer Stanhope, 4th Earl of Chesterfield, was a well-known British politician, diplomat, and man of literature. He was blessed with a rich childhood and an education that included a Grand Tour of Europe when he was born in 1694. As a courtier to King George I, Chesterfield joined politics before rising to the position of member of the House of Commons and then the House of Lords. Chesterfield held a number of political posts and was well known for his oratory in the House of Lords. He was also known for his eloquence and diplomatic abilities. Chesterfield was active in humanitarian work and the advancement of academic interests in addition to his political career. He made a substantial contribution to the Foundling Hospital's foundation and helped Britain adopt the Gregorian calendar. Although renowned for his humor and brilliance, Samuel Johnson and Chesterfield had a tense relationship as a result of their differences on the release of Johnson's dictionary. Chesterfield increasingly left politics in his latter years as a result of his deteriorating health and worsening hearing loss. He criticized the Stamp Act of 1765, pointing out its unfeasibility and possible negative economic effects on the American colonies. As a politician, diplomat, and author, Philip Dormer Stanhope, 4th Earl of Chesterfield, left behind an enduring legacy.

CONTENTS

Chapter-I.

Philip Dormer Stanhope did not experience in his youth either of those influences which are so important in the lives of most of us. His mother died before he could know her, and his father was one of those living nonentities whom his biographer sums up in saying that "We know little more of him than that he was an Earl of Chesterfield." Indeed, what influence there may have been was of a negative kind, for he had, if anything, an avowed dislike for his son. Naturally under these conditions he had to endure the slings and arrows of fortune alone and uncounselled. One domestic influence was allowed him in the mother of his mother, whose face still looks out at us from the pages of Dr. Maty, engraved by Bartolozzi from the original of Sir Peter Lely — a face sweet, intellectual, open — over the title of Gertrude Savile, Marchioness of Halifax. She it was who undertook, at any rate to some small degree, the rearing of her daughter's child. Lord Chesterfield is rather a Savile than a Stanhope.

He heard French from a Normandy nurse in his cradle, and he received, when he grew a little older, "such a general idea of the sciences as it is a disgrace to a gentleman not to possess." But it is not till he gets to Cambridge at the age of eighteen that we hear anything definite. He writes to his tutor of former days, whom he seems to have made a real friend, from Trinity Hall:

> "I find the college where I am infinitely the best in the university; for it is the smallest, and filled with lawyers who have lived in the world, and know how to behave. Whatever may be said to the contrary, there is certainly very little debauchery in the university, especially amongst people of fashion, for a man must have the inclinations of a porter to endure it here."

Thirty-six years later he draws for his son this picture of his college-life:

> "As I make no difficulty of confessing my past errors, where I think the confession may be of use to you, I will own that, when I first went to the university, I drank and smoked, notwithstanding the aversion I had to wine and tobacco, only because I thought it genteel, and that it made me look a man."

This touch of nature it is interesting to find in one who gave so much to the Graces. But to get at what he really did we may take the following:

"It is now, Sir, I have a great deal of business upon my hands; for I spend an hour every day in studying civil law, and as much in philosophy; and next week the blind man [Dr. Sanderson] begins his lectures upon the mathematics; so that I am now fully employed. Would you believe, too, that I read Lucian and Xenophon in Greek, which is made easy to me; for I do not take the pains to learn the grammatical rules; but the gentleman who is with me, and who is a living grammar, teaches me them all as I go along. I reserve time for playing at tennis, for I wish to have the *corpus sanum* as well as the *mens sana*: I think the one is not good for much without the other. As for anatomy, I shall not have an opportunity of learning it; for though a poor man has been hanged, the surgeon who used to perform those operations would not this year give any lectures, because, he says, ... the scholars will not come.

"Methinks our affairs are in a very bad way, but as I cannot mend them, I meddle very little in politics; only I take a pleasure in going sometimes to the coffee house to see the pitched battles that are fought between the heroes of each party with inconceivable bravery, and are usually terminated by the total defeat of a few tea-cups on both sides."2

He only stayed in Cambridge two years, and then travelled abroad to Flanders and Holland. He had just left The Hague when the news reached him across the water which only then was not stale — Queen Anne was dead.

It was the turning point of his career, for his great-uncle, who had influence and position at the court, obtained for him from George I. the post of Gentleman of the Bedchamber to the Prince of Wales. At the same time he obtained a pocket-borough in Cornwall, and appeared in the House of Commons. He was not yet of age, of which fact a friend in the opposition politely and quietly informed him after he had made his first speech. He was, therefore, not only debarred from voting, but liable to a fine of £500. He made a low bow, left the House, and posted straightway to Paris.

He was not there long. Advancing months soon removed the objection of age, and we find him again frequently in the House. His position on the Schism and Occasional Conformity Bills was one which he himself in after years regretted. He was still, however, swimming with the stream, and the stream led on to fortune. In 1723 he was made Captain of the Yeomen of the Guards, and two years later, when the Order of the Bath was revived, was offered by the King the red ribbon. But this he refused; and not contented with so much discourtesy, objected to others accepting it. He wrote a ballad on Sir William Morgan, who had received the same offer. The ballad came to the ears of the King; and for this, or for other reasons, Stanhope the courtier lost his place.

At this juncture two changes took place, to him of equal importance. George I. died and brought Stanhope's former master to the throne; and Lord Chesterfield died, leaving his son his title. The latter event raised him to the House of Lords — the Hospital for Incurables, as Lord Chesterfield calls it. The former should have raised him to higher office still; but that policy of scheming for which Lord Chesterfield has become almost as famous as Macchiavelli in this case played him false. Believing that where marriage begins, love, as a necessary consequence, ends, he had paid all his attentions to the new King's mistress, while he was still Prince of Wales, and none to his queen. And Caroline of Anspach took precaution that when George II. came to the throne the courtier's negligence should be treated as it deserved. Thus at the age of thirty-three, while still a young man, Chesterfield was cut off from the Court: and he was already in opposition to Walpole. The King as a subterfuge offered him the post of Ambassador to Holland, and the offended courtier was thus removed. But political events were moving rapidly, and in two years' time it was rumored that Chesterfield would be reinstated in favor. The King, however, was still obdurate, and instead of Secretary of State he was made High Steward of the Household. Chesterfield remained in Holland, gambling and watching events. "I find treating with two hundred sovereigns of different tempers and professions," he writes, "is as laborious as treating with one fine woman, who is at least of two hundred minds in one day."

The game went on for a year more. Then he was by his own wish recalled. On the 2d of May of this same year he was presented with a son by Mme. Du Bouchet. "A beautiful young lady at The Hague," says one writer, "set her wits against his and suffered the usual penalty; she fell, and this son was the result." This son was the object of all Lord Chesterfield's care and affection. It was to him that his now famous letters were written. The father, we find, on his return to England, in the House talking indefatigably as ever. It was the year of Walpole's Excise Bill which was to have freed the country by changing the system of taxation from direct to indirect methods. It was a good measure and a just one. Every part of Walpole's scheme has been since carried into effect. But then there was a general cry raised against it. The liberties of the people, it was said, were being attacked. Chesterfield, with the rest of the Patriots, and with the country behind them, fought hard, and the Bill was dropped (11th April, 1731). Two days afterward, going up the steps of St. James' Palace, he was stopped by a servant in the livery of the Duke of Grafton, who told him that his master must see him immediately. He drove off at once in the Duke's carriage, and found that he was to surrender the White Staff. He demanded an audience at Court, obtained it, and was snubbed. Of course he left it immediately.

We could have wished perhaps that Lord Chesterfield's affection and character had prevented him from falling — especially so soon after the affair at The Hague — into so unpraiseworthy an undertaking as a *mariage de convenance*. Yet whether it was to spite his royal enemy, or because in financial difficulties he remembered the existence of the will of George I. — or even from love; at any rate in the following year he married, in lawful wedlock, Melusina de Schulenberg, whom, though merely the "niece" of the Duchess of Kendale, George the First had thought fit to create Lady Walsingham and the possessor by his will of £20,000. Scandal or truth has been very busy about the relationship of Lady Walsingham and her aunt. Posterity openly declares her to have been the daughter of that lady by a royal sire. But good Dr. Maty, as though by the quantity of his information, wishing to override its quality, tells us that her father was none other than one "Frederick Achatz de Schulenburg, privy counsellor to the Duke of Brunswick-Lunenburg, Lord of Stehler, Bezendorff, Angern," etc. But we may well remember Lord Chesterfield's own words here: "It is a happy phrase that a lady has presented her husband with a son, for this does not admit anything of its parentage." Anyhow Lord Chesterfield lost the money, for George the Second, on being shown his father's will by the Archbishop of Canterbury, put it in his pocket and walked hastily out of the room. It never was seen again.

But to have quarrelled with George II. had one recommendation. It made him a friend of the Prince of Wales. No sooner was Lord Chesterfield married than the Prince and Princess sent round their cards, and the rest of their Court, of course, followed them. It seems to have been Lord Chesterfield's fate to be opposed to the reigning power. His opposition now, however, was quite spontaneous.

We need not follow him through all the political entanglements of the time. Smollet said of him that he was the only man of genius employed under Walpole, and though history has hardly justified such praise, yet it certainly illustrates a truth. We may take his speech in 1737 against the Playhouse Bill as a sample of his oratory. I borrow from Lord Mahon:

"[The speech] contains many eloquent predictions, that, should the Bill be enacted, the ruin of liberty and the introduction of despotism would inevitably follow. Yet even Chesterfield owns that 'he has observed of late a remarkable licentiousness in the stage. In one play very lately acted (Pasquin3) the author thought fit to represent the three great professions, religion, physic, and law as inconsistent with common sense; in another (King Charles the First4), a most tragical story was brought upon the stage — a catastrophe too recent, too melancholy, and of too solemn a nature, to be heard of anywhere but from the pulpit. How these pieces came to pass unpunished, I do not know.... The Bill, my Lords, may seem to be designed only against the stage; but to me it plainly appears to point somewhere else. It is an arrow that does but glance upon the stage: the mortal wound seems designed against the liberty of the press. By this Bill you prevent a play's being acted, but you do not prevent it being printed. Therefore if a license should be refused for its being acted, we may depend upon it the play will be printed. It will be printed and published, my Lords, with the refusal, in capital letters, upon the title-page. People are always fond of what is forbidden. *Libri prohibiti* are, in all countries, diligently and generally sought after. It will be much easier to procure a refusal than it ever was to procure a good house or a good sale; therefore we may expect that plays will be wrote on purpose to have a refusal; this will certainly procure a good house or a good sale. Thus will satires be spread and dispersed through the whole nation; and thus every man in the kingdom may, and probably will, read for sixpence what a few only could have seen acted for half a crown. We shall then be told, What! will you allow an infamous libel to be printed and dispersed, which you will not allow to be acted? If we agree to the Bill now before us, we must, perhaps, next session, agree to a Bill for preventing any plays being printed without a license. Then satires will be wrote by way of novels, secret histories, dialogues, or under some such title; and thereupon we shall be told, What! will you allow an infamous libel to be printed and dispersed, only because it does not bear the title of a play? Thus, my Lords, from the precedent now before us, we shall be induced, nay, we can find no reason for refusing, to lay the press under a general license, and then we may bid adieu to the liberties of Great Britain.'"5 Of course it is impossible from single passages, even perhaps from single speeches, to infer that he was ever a great orator, but Horace Walpole has declared one of his speeches the finest that he had ever listened to, and, as Lord Mahon justly observes, "Horace Walpole had heard his own father; had heard Pitt; had heard Pulteney; had heard Windham; had heard Carteret; yet he declares in 1743 that the finest speech he had ever listened to was one from Lord Chesterfield."

He was, with the other "Patriots," in clamoring for war with Spain, pursuing Walpole with an opposition which has been characterized as "more factious and unprincipled than any that had ever disgraced English politics" (Green). In 1739, it will be remembered, Walpole bowed to the storm. The following extract from *An Ode to a Number of Great Men*, published in 1742, will show underneath its virulence who were expected to take the lead:

"But first to C[arteret] fain you'd sing,
Indeed he's nearest to the king,
Yet careless how to use him,

Give him, I beg, no labor'd lays,
He will but promise if you praise,
And laugh if you abuse him.

"Then (but there's a vast space betwixt)
The new-made E[arl] of B[ath] comes next,
Stiff in his popular pride:
His step, his gait describe the man,
They paint him better than I can,
Wabbling from side to side.

"Each hour a different face he wears,
Now in a fury, now in tears,
Now laughing, now in sorrow,
Now he'll command, and now obey,
Bellows for liberty to-day,
And roars for power to-morrow.

"At noon the Tories had him tight,
With staunchest Whigs he supped at night,
Each party thought to have won him:
But he himself did so divide,
Shuffled and cut from side to side,
That now both parties shun him.

"More changes, better times this isle
Demands, oh! Chesterfield, Argyll,
To bleeding Britain bring 'em;
Unite all hearts, appease each storm,
'Tis yours such actions to perform,
My pride shall be to sing 'em."

Affairs in Holland again compelled him to seek that Court, and it is thence that he was summoned to Ireland in 1744. "Make Chenevix an Irish Bishop," he had written. "We cannot," was the reply, "but any other condition." "Then make me Lord-Lieutenant," he wrote back. They took him at his word, and Chenevix soon obtained his place.

Chesterfield had always looked forward to the post with longing. "I would rather be called the Irish Lord-Lieutenant," he had said, "than go down to Posterity as the Lord-Lieutenant of Ireland." It was, as has been truly observed, the most brilliant and useful part of his career. I shall be pardoned for quoting again from Mahon. "It was he who first, since the revolution, had made that office a post of active exertion. Only a few years before the Earl of Shrewsbury had given as a reason for accepting it, that it was a place where a man had business enough to hinder him from falling asleep, and not enough to keep him awake. Chesterfield, on the contrary, left nothing undone nor for others to do.... [He] was the first to introduce in Dublin the principle of impartial justice. It is very easy, as was formerly the case, to choose the great Protestant families as managers; to see only through their eyes, and to hear only through their ears; it is very easy, according to the modern fashion, to become the tool and the champion of Roman Catholic agitators; but to hold the balance even between both; to protect the Establishment, yet never wound religious liberty; to repress the lawlessness, yet not chill the affection of that turbulent but warm-hearted people; to be the arbiter, not the slave of parties; this is the true object worthy that a statesman should strive for, and fit only for the ablest to attain! 'I came determined,' writes Chesterfield many years afterward, 'to proscribe no set of persons whatever; and determined to be governed by none. Had the Papists made any attempt to put themselves above the law, I should have taken good care to have quelled them again. It was said that my lenity to the Papists had wrought no alteration, either in their religion or political sentiments. I did not expect that it would; but surely there was no reason of cruelty toward them.'... So able were the measures of Chesterfield; so clearly did he impress upon the public mind that his moderation was not weakness, nor his clemency cowardice, but that, to quote his own words, 'his hand should be as heavy as Cromwell's upon them if they once forced him to raise it.' So well did he know how to scare the timid, while conciliating the generous, that this alarming period [1745] passed over with a degree of tranquillity such as Ireland has not often displayed even in orderly and settled times. This just and wise — wise because just — administration has not failed to reward him with its meed of fame; his authority has, I find, been appealed to even by those who, as I conceive, depart most widely from his maxims; and his name, I am assured, lives in the honored remembrance of the Irish people, as perhaps, next to Ormond, the best and worthiest in their long Viceregal line."

We know that it was a complete success, so far as it went. But he held the post only for four years. He had held the highest offices, he had attained his highest wishes; yet his membership in the Cabinet had been made nominal rather than real, and his power was ever controlled by the hand of the King. Nowhere, in whatever direction he might care to turn his eyes along the political landscape, could he see anything but what was rotten and revolting. In 1748 he retired.

We cannot call his political career an unsuccessful one. It was probably as brilliant as it was possible for a man of his parts to enjoy. He was a good talker and an incomparable ambassador. His action in Holland had permanent influence on the politics of Europe. But indeed, if he had been freed from the opposition of a profligate Court and all that it entailed; if, as has been implied by some, he would have been a greater man had not the death of his father driven him into the House of Lords; if he would then have risen to be anything greater than a second-rate Minister: this we may doubt. Yet we are not entitled to draw an estimate of his character before we have studied its other side.

Chesterfield did not entirely give up attendance or even speaking at the House, but his energies henceforward were devoted to literary rather than political matters. One further act he performed before he left for good; he carried out three years later the reform of the English Calendar, an account of which he gives in one of his letters, and I cannot equal his words.6 This was the last important public event in his life. Next year he was attacked with deafness, which incapacitated him of necessity from affairs. It does not seem that he was ever sorry to leave them. Ever and anon the old political fire breaks out, and we find him keeping an observant eye on the course of events. But he was thoroughly despondent of the prestige and ascendancy of England by the time of the outbreak of the Seven Years' War. "Nation!" he had cried, "we are no longer a nation." We find him sympathizing with Wilkes, and to the end on the side of Pitt. But about 1765 his letters begin to bear the mark of decrepitude, and his brains to be unable to cope with the situations that arose.

> "I see and hear these storms from shore, *suave mari magno, &c.* I enjoy my own security and tranquillity, together with better health than I have reason to expect at my age and with my constitution: however, I feel a gradual decay, though a gentle one; and I think I shall not tumble, but slide gently to the bottom of the hill of life. When that will be I neither know nor care, for I am very weary."

And in the following August, anticipating alike the autumn of his life and of the year, he writes:

> "I feel this beginning of the autumn, which is already very cold; the leaves are withered, fall apace, and seem to intimate that I must follow them, which I shall do without reluctance, being extremely weary of this silly world." — (Letter CCCLV.)

Yet even a year later we find him giving dinner parties to the Duke of Brunswick, and wishing that he had both the monarchs of Austria and Prussia, that they should, "together with some of their allies, take Lorraine and Alsace from France." (Letter CCCLXIV.) For a few more years he lingered on, gardening, reading, and writing, and then in 1773, almost alone, he parted with "this silly world."

Chapter-II.

I have omitted from this sketch of Lord Chesterfield's political life any reference to the literary side of his character. I have, however, spoken of his friendship with Voltaire. Voltaire came to England in the same year that Chesterfield's father died, to obtain, among other things, a publisher for the *Henriade*. Chesterfield and Bolingbroke at once took him up and introduced him into high places.7 Voltaire never forgot him nor the services which he had rendered; and one of the most charming lights thrown upon the end of Lord Chesterfield's career is in a letter from the old sage of Ferney to his friend of younger days, now grown old as himself. Chesterfield was always a great admirer of Voltaire's, though by no means a blind one:

> "I strongly doubt," he writes, "whether it is permissible for a man to write against the worship and belief of his country, even if he be fully persuaded of its error, on account of the terrible trouble and disorder it might cause; but I am sure it is in no wise allowable to attack the foundations of true morality, and to break unnecessary bonds which are already too weak to keep men in the path of duty."

But differences upon points of morality and religion did not prevent his having an immense regard for Voltaire's genius.

There is yet the other transaction in which Lord Chesterfield was engaged, and it will probably be as long remembered against him as the letters—his ill-famed treatment of Dr. Johnson. It is too well known how Johnson came to his door, and how Chesterfield, who could never be impolite, received the ill-mannered Doctor. But either the Earl objected to having the old man annoying his guests at table, or else he was not sufficiently pressing with his money; anyhow, the Doctor felt repelled, left off calling, and never sought another patron. Years afterward, when he brought out his Dictionary (1755), there was a letter prefixed to the first edition, entitled "The Blast of Doom, proclaiming that patronage shall be no more." Boswell solicited the Doctor for many years to give him a copy, but he did not do so until 1781, and then gave it from memory:

> "... Seven years, my lord, have passed since I waited in your outward rooms, or was repulsed from your door; during which time I have been pushing on my work under difficulties,

of which it is useless to complain, and have brought it to the verge of publication without one act of assistance, one word of encouragement, or one smile of favor. Such treatment I did not expect; for I never had a patron before....

"Is not a patron, my lord, one who looks with unconcern on a man struggling for life in the water, and, when he has reached ground, encumbers him with help? The notice you have been pleased to take of my labors, had it been early, had been kind; but it has been delayed till I am indifferent, and cannot enjoy it; till I am solitary and cannot impart it; till I am known and do not want it. I hope it is no very cynical asperity not to confess obligations, where no benefit has been received; or to be unwilling that the public should consider me as owing that to a patron which providence has enabled me to do for myself.

"Having carried on my work thus far, with so little obligation to any favorer of learning, I shall not be disappointed, though I should conclude it, if possible, with less; for I have been long wakened from that dream of hope in which I once boasted myself with so much exaltation, my lord, your lordship's most humble and most obedient servant,

"Samuel Johnson."

Such a transaction is but little to the praise of Lord Chesterfield, who would have posed as the Mæcenas of the eighteenth century. But there the matter rests. It is another proof of what the Earl was not, but with the slightest bend of his body might have been. He lost the Dedication to one of the greatest achievements of the time.

Chapter-III.

Let us turn to Lord Chesterfield's son. Sainte-Beuve says of him — he was "one of those ordinary men of the world of whom it suffices to say there is nothing to be said." But there is so much melancholy interest attaching to his history that we may well try to discern some of the features of the youth. No portrait of Philip Stanhope, so far as I am aware, has ever been given to the public, though we know from his father's letters that one, if not more than one, was executed at Venice during his stay there, so that I am unable, as yet, to surmise anything from physical feature of form and angle. We know that his father sent him to Westminster School, and that there he was slovenly and dirty. Of his intellectual qualities we hear nothing. His father's letter to the boy, then sixteen, is subtle:

> "Since you do not care to be an Assessor of the Imperial Chamber, and desire an establishment in England, what do you think of being Greek Professor at one of our Universities? It is a very pretty sinecure, and requires very little knowledge (much less than, I hope, you have already) of that language. If you do not approve of this, I am at a loss to know what else to propose to you."

The old earl, six months later, added as follows:

> "The end I propose by your education, and which (*if you please*) I shall certainly attain, is, to unite in you all the knowledge of a scholar, with the manners of a courtier, and to join what is seldom joined in any of my countrymen, Books and the World. They are commonly twenty years old before they have spoken to anybody above their schoolmaster, and the Fellows of their College. If they happen to have learning, it is only Greek and Latin; but not one word of Modern History or Modern Languages. Thus prepared, they go abroad, as they call it; but, in truth, they stay at home all that while; for, being very awkward, confoundedly ashamed, and not speaking the languages, they go into no foreign company, at least none good, but dine and sup with one another at the tavern. Such example, I am sure you will not imitate, but carefully avoid."

Young Stanhope went abroad with a tutor, Mr. Harte, to the chief towns, first, of Germany, followed everywhere by letters from his father, though, as his father says in one of them, "God knows whether to any purpose or not." He never escaped from the paternal care. Wherever you are "I have Arguses with a hundred eyes," his father told him. The boy was affectionately fond of his father, though he did not inherit his father's epistolary taste. Yet we find him on corresponding terms with Lady Chesterfield. He was inclined to be stout, a fault which his father tells him to remedy by abstaining from Teutonic beer. He wore long hair. "I by no means agree to your cutting off your hair." (Stanhope had suggested this as a remedy for headaches.) "Your own hair is at your age such an ornament; and a wig, however well made, such a disguise that I will upon no account whatever have you cut off your hair." We hear that he was already within two inches of his father's height. Boswell met him at Dresden, and has left us the following picture of him:—"Mr. Stanhope's character has been unjustly represented as being diametrically opposed to what Lord Chesterfield wished him to be. He has been called dull, gross, awkward, but I knew him at Dresden when he was envoy to that Court, and though he could not boast of the Graces, he was, in fact, a sensible, civil, well-behaved man." And what he was as envoy he seems to have been all his life. Lord Chesterfield sent him to Berlin first,8 and Turin afterward, as there was to be found the next fittest training in Europe at that Court. Nothing could exceed his father's care in warning him against such dangers as usually attend Court life. Against evils of all kind he cautions and guards him. Yet there is this continual insistence on the Graces. "The Graces! The Graces!" he writes, "Remember the Graces! I would have you sacrifice to the Graces." By no means must a man neglect the Graces if he would pursue his object, the object of getting on.

After all this schooling he went to Paris, and seems to have made a tolerable *début*. There must have been a strange measuring up of qualities when father and son met. At twenty-two Lord Chesterfield obtained for him a seat in the House, but he was never a brilliant speaker. He, like the younger Pitt, was a parliamentary experiment; but it was not given to Stanhope to succeed. In 1757 he goes to Hamburg. Two years later his health broke down, and he came to England. But feeling better again, in 1763 he obtained a post at Ratisbon, whence he was once summoned to vote in the English Parliament. Next year he went to Dresden as envoy, but there his constitution was ruined, and he set off for Berlin, and afterward for France. In the spring of 1767 he returned to Dresden, fancying himself better, but in the following year the old symptoms returned, and he died on the 17th of October, 1768, near Avignon. It was then only that his father discovered he was the father of two children—by a secret marriage. And these, together with their mother, were thrown upon Lord Chesterfield for support. It is one of the examples of his characteristic traits that he supported and loved all three. There is no more charming pendant to the whole series of letters than a short one of three paragraphs which he wrote to the two children of his illegitimate son only two years before he left them forever.

Here my biographical notice of the three generations ends. But the lives of father and son will ever remain full of interest and suggestion to those who would study human character.

There are several portraits of the Earl of Chesterfield. The most striking, and at the same time probably the most faithful which we have, is that by Bartolozzi in the *Maty Memoirs*. It is clear, mobile, and benevolent. The features are very large, and the eyes of that cold meditative species which look as though they were the altar stone of that fire of wit and quaint humor which we know he possessed. It is a fine intellectual, if somewhat too receding, forehead, with protruding temples and clear-cut eyebrows; the nose prominent, and the mouth pronounced. There is a great diversity however in the portraits, and he seems sometimes to have been unable to hide the traits of sensuality. Yet, on the whole, it is as inscrutable as his own scheming diplomatic soul could ever have wished for its earthly representative in clay.

Chapter-IV.

If we ask ourselves what is the moral of the Letters, and what is their significance, we are met with a varied reply. We have here the outpourings of a man's soul *in penetralibus.* As such the book stands for its time unique. Chesterfield, when he wrote these letters, was not actuated by the criticisms of Grub Street, nor indeed any criticisms. He never for a moment dreamt that his letters would be published, and they are therefore bereft of that stifling self-consciousness which is the bane of so many writers. It is this which makes so frequently a man's letters more living than his published works, at any rate more real. So far, of course, Lord Chesterfield shares this distinction with other writers. But his letters are noteworthy for more than this. They combine with it a complete system of education, a system which was thought out without opposition and expressed without fear. In such a case, of course, we do not look for style; but so perfect and so equal was the man that we are even told that these letters are not exceeded in style by anything in the language.9

Manuals, of course, there have been many. In the age gone by there had been Walsingham's, there had been Burghley's *Advice,* there had been Sir Walter Raleigh's; but from the time that Cicero wrote his *De Officiis* for his own child down to these, we come upon but few of this sort. There had been Castiglione's *Cortegiano,* and in a few years Della Casa's *Galateo;* there is Roger Ascham's *Scholemaster.* Chesterfield had found much to his taste and method in the *Moral Reflections* of La Rochefoucauld and the *Characters* of La Bruyère. In England had just appeared Locke's *Essay on Education,* and this he sends for his son to read.10 In 1759 Lessing and Wieland were writing on the same subject; and in 1762 Rousseau published *Emile.* Everywhere education was, to use a common phrase, in the air. Chesterfield loved his son passionately and unremittingly. He had been much in France, and admired the French nation; and he determined that his son should combine the good qualities of both nationalities—the ideal statesman and the ideal polished man of society. He did not forget that on Philip Stanhope would ever remain the brand of the bar sinister; but we may well believe that this was only one more daring reason for the experiment which he chose to make. He was playing for high stakes, and he was not careless of the issue. "My only ambition," he writes in 1754, "remaining is to be the counsellor and minister of your rising ambition. Let me see my own youth revived in you; let me be your mentor, and I promise you, with your parts and knowledge you shall go far." — (Letter CCLXXIV.)

It is seldom that we have such a continuous series of original letters as these. From the first *badinage* to his son, then five years old, who was then in Holland, in which he explains what a republic is, and how clean is Holland in comparison with London; from the times when he explains how Poetry is made, and who the Muses are, and sends his little son accounts of all the Greek and Roman legends; from the times when he writes, "Let us return to our Geography that we may amuse ourselves with maps;" and in the middle of a letter of affection, having mentioned Cicero, starts off "apropos of him," and gives his little son his whole history, and that of Demosthenes after him; to the times when the boy is able to retort on him for inconsistency in calling Ovidius Ovid, and not calling Tacitus Tacit; through all his explanations of what Irony is and is not; through his pedantic "by the ways;" his definitions (*pace* Professor Freeman) of Ancient and Modern History; his sarcasms and his descriptions: down to the time when his advice is about quadrille tables and ministers and kings, the series is absolutely unbroken and of unflagging interest.

They are at the best, as he says himself, "what one man of the world writes to another." "I am not writing poetry," he says, "but useful reflections." "Surely it is of great use to a young man before he starts out for a country full of mazes, windings and turnings, to have at least a good map of it by some experienced traveller." And so the old man gives us his map of life as he had seen it. It is exactly the same estimate in result as Cicero gave in the *De Oratore*: "Men judge most things under the influence of either hate, or love, or desire, or anger, or grief, or joy, or hope, or fear, or error, or some other passion, than by truth, or precepts, or standard of right, or justice, or law."

"The proper study of mankind is man,"

and if we disapprove of the morality of Cicero and his epoch no less than of Chesterfield's, we must yet remember that in the one instance, as in the other, their precepts were the purveyors of very soundest advice. His standard is, as has been already pointed out, that of the eighteenth century. "Be wiser than other people if you can; but do not tell them so." "It is an active, cheerful, seducing good breeding which must gain you the good-will and first sentiments of the men and affections of the women. You must carefully watch and attend to their passions, their tastes, their little humors and weaknesses, and *aller au devant*." "Make love to the most impertinent beauty that you meet with, and be gallant with all the rest."

It would be a not uninteresting task to see how many of his moral sentiments would stand fire at the present day. We know all the facts of his life, and we have here his opinions on nearly every matter. His opinions are as concise as they are outspoken. "The best of us have had our bad sides, and it is as imprudent as it is ill-bred to exhibit them,"11 he says. It is this absence of ceremony which makes him so living and real. Even in Dr. Johnson's time the merit as well as the demerit of this series of letters had been settled for the standard of that day. "Take out the immorality," said the worthy Doctor, "and it should be put into the hands of every young gentleman."

The training to which he subjected his son was in many ways admirable. Rise regularly, however late o' nights; work all the morning; take exercise in the afternoon; and see good company in the evening. The impressing of this advice upon his son has left us in the possession of one of the most charming examples of Lord Chesterfield's most playful style. — (Letter CLXI.)

Lord Chesterfield was all for modern to the disadvantage of a classical education. Learn all the modern history and modern languages you can, and if at the same time you can throw in a little Latin and Greek, so much the better for you. Roman history study as much as you will, for of all ancient histories it is the most instructive, and furnishes most examples of virtue, wisdom, and courage. History is to be studied morally, he says, but not *only* so.

When we turn to his judgment of the ancients we are considerably startled. He seems to have preferred Voltaire's *Henriade* to any epic. "Judge whether," he writes, "I can read all Homer through *tout de suite*. I admire his beauties; but, to tell you the truth, when he slumbers I sleep. Virgil, I confess, is all sense, and therefore I like him better than his model; but he is often languid, especially in his five or six last books, during which I am obliged to take a good deal of snuff...."

If his views on Milton should be known, he adds, he would be abused by every tasteless pedant and every solid divine in England. His criticism of Dante it will be best for the reader to discover.

The weightier questions and the weightiest he pushed altogether aside. "I don't speak of religion," he writes. "I am not in a position to do so — the excellent Mr. Harte will do that." At any rate, Chesterfield knew his own ground. Incidentally we find his position cropping up. "The reason of every man is, or ought to be, his guide; and I should have as much right to expect every man to be of my height and temperament as to wish that he should reason precisely as I do." It was the doctrine of the French school that he had adopted, with something of a quietism of his own. "Let them enjoy quietly their errors," he says somewhere, "both in taste and religion."12 It would be interesting to compare in these matters the relative positions of Chesterfield and Bolingbroke.

Of the movement headed by Wesley, as we have seen earlier in his career, Chesterfield seems to have taken as little heed as the younger Pliny did of the first holders of Wesley's faith.

It is a harder and more delicate question which we are met with in discussing Lord Chesterfield's position with regard to morality. Johnson's criticism of the *Letters*, that "they taught the morals of a courtesan and manners of a dancing master," even though epigrammatic, yet bears within it traces of the sting which the lexicologist felt about the matter of the Dedication. Of the Earl's opinions we have seen something in former extracts and in his own life. He speaks quite openly — "I wish to speak as one man of pleasure does to another." "A polite arrangement," he says elsewhere, "becomes a gallant man." Anything disgraceful or impolite he will not stand.

Yet as a human Picciola does Lord Chesterfield guard the soul of his son within its prison-house of life. He never speaks, however, to his son *pulpitically*. It is ever as a wise counsellor: and his tendency is always the same.

It is suggestive of much to turn aside from the *petitesses* of these instructions to the thoughts which were occupying the brain of the author of *Emilius* about the same time. From very much the same foundations and the same materials how different is the result! In the one we breathe the fresh air of the country, of the rustic home and the carpenter's shop: in the other we are stifled by the perfumes of the court-room and suffocated by tight lacing. In the one we are never for a moment to wear a mask: in the other we are never for a moment to move without it. Yet, though the one is built up of social theories by an enthusiastic dreamer, and the other is a cold, practical experiment by a man of the world, and "an imperfect man of action, whom politics had made a perfect moralist," there is the same verdict of failure to be pronounced upon them both. Voltaire said of *Emilius* that it was a stupid romance, but admitted that it contained fifty pages which he would have bound in morocco. Lord Chesterfield's was no romance, but its pages deserve perhaps as careful treatment. "It is a rich book," says Sainte-Beuve; "one cannot read a page without finding some happy observation worthy of being mentioned." Yet, as a system of education, it is blasted with the foul air of the charnel-house.

Chapter-V.

If we look at the result we must pronounce his experiment no less a failure. The odds were too heavy in the first instance, and a man of less energy and stability than Lord Chesterfield would not have dared to have played at such high stakes. He ought to have considered what an infliction he was casting upon his son, and respected the feelings of others rather than his own ambition. He has reaped the harvest which he had sown. When Philip Stanhope tried to obtain an appointment at the embassy in Brussels the Marquis de Botta made so much to do on the ground of his illegitimacy that his claim was disallowed. When there was a chance of his receiving an appointment at Venice, the king objected on the same grounds. Not one word of displeasure is handed down to us in these familiar letters, but we know that both felt it deeply and never forgave. But even Philip Stanhope himself must have disappointed his father. When his widow, with her two children, walked up the hall of Chesterfield House, where the Earl sat alone in solitary childless grandeur, it must have seemed a strange answer to the question which he had asked Time some thirty-eight years before. He may well have grown weary of sitting at the table at which he had staked his all and lost.

Vivacious, sincere, plain, and liberal-minded, his memory may well pass down to posterity as that of a great man with mean aspirations. That ambition was not wanting in his composition is true, and it was this which encompassed his ruin. He reminds us of the melancholy structure of S. Petronio at Bologna, begun in emulation of the Florentine Duomo by the Bolognese. One sees the outline of the structure which was to have been raised, but for two centuries it has stood uncompleted, a monument to her greatness and her shame.

Careless of the interests of those around him; careless and callous of what was demanded of man by men; careless of speech so long as he could create a *bon mot* or a well-balanced phrase, Lord Chesterfield's life is characteristic of his time.

Chesterfield, if we may make one more comparison, is like one of those great trees that we see upon the banks of a river, which, while drawing its nurture half from its native soil and the stream by its side, and half from the sky above it, has had that very soil worn away by the current of the stream, so that the tree, by its own natural weight and under the force of adverse winds and circumstance, has bowed itself over toward the waves, losing its natural height and grandeur for ever.

Dead to the higher interests of humanity; dead to the deeper influences which keep us sober and thoughtful and earnest; dead, again, to any ideal save such as might serve his own designs:—such was the man who deemed himself called upon, or fitted, to perform the sacred office of Education to his darling child.

CRITICAL ESSAY.

BY C. A. SAINTE-BEUVE.[13]

Each epoch has produced its treatise intended for the formation of the *polite man*, the man *of the world*, the *courtier*, when men only lived for courts, and the accomplished *gentleman*. In these various treatises on knowledge of life and politeness, if opened after a lapse of ages, we at once see portions which are as antiquated as the cut and fashion of our forefathers' coats; the *model* has evidently changed. But looking into it carefully as a whole, if the book has been written by a sensible man with a true knowledge of mankind, we shall find profit in studying these models which have been placed before preceding generations. The letters that Lord Chesterfield wrote to his son, and which contain a whole school of *savoir vivre* and worldly science, are interesting in this particular, that there has been no idea of forming a model for imitation, but they are simply intended to bring up a pupil in the closest intimacy. They are confidential letters, which, suddenly produced in the light of day, have betrayed all the secrets and ingenious artifices of paternal solicitude. If, in reading them nowadays, we are struck with the excessive importance attached to accidental and promiscuous circumstances, with pure details of costume, we are not less struck with the durable part, with that which belongs to human observation in all ages; and this last part is much more considerable than at a superficial glance would be imagined. In applying himself to the formation of his son as a *polite man* in society, Lord Chesterfield has not given us a treatise on *duty* as Cicero has; but he has left letters which, by their mixture of justness and lightness, by certain lightsome airs which insensibly mingle with the serious graces, preserve the medium between the *Mémoires of the Chevalier de Grammont* and *Télémaque*.

Before going into detail, it will be necessary to know a little about Lord Chesterfield, one of the most brilliant English wits of his time, and one most closely allied to France. Philip Dormer Stanhope, Earl of Chesterfield, was born in London on the 22d of September, 1694, the same year as Voltaire. The descendant of an illustrious race, he knew the value of birth, and wished to sustain its honor; nevertheless, it was difficult for him not to laugh at genealogical pretensions when carried too far. To keep himself from this folly, he had placed amongst the portraits of his ancestors two old figures of a man and a woman: beneath one was written, "*Adam* de Stanhope"; and beneath the other "*Eve* de Stanhope." Thus, while upholding the honor of race, he put his veto upon chimerical vanities arising from it.

His father paid no attention whatever to his education; he was placed under the care of his grandmother, Lady Halifax. From a very early age he manifested a desire to excel in everything, a desire which later he did his utmost to excite in the breast of his son, and which for good or ill is the principle of all that is great. It appears that, in his early youth, he was without guidance, he was deceived more than once in the objects of his emulation, and followed some ridiculous chimera. He confesses that at one period of inexperience he gave himself up to wine, and other excesses, for which he was not at all inclined by nature, but it flattered his vanity to hear himself cited as a man of pleasure. In this way he plunged into play (which he considered a necessary ingredient in the composition of a young man of fashion), at first without passion, but afterwards without being able to withdraw himself from it, and by that means compromised his fortune for years. "Take warning by my conduct," said he to his son, "choose your own pleasures, and do not let others choose them for you."

The desire to excel and to distinguish himself did not always lead him astray, and he often applied it rightly; his first studies were the best. Placed at the University of Cambridge, he studied all that was there taught, civil law and philosophy; he attended the mathematical classes of Saunderson, the blind professor, he read Greek fluently, and sent accounts of his progress in French to his old tutor, M. Jouneau, a French clergyman and refugee. Lord Chesterfield had, when a child, learnt our tongue from a Norman nurse who attended him. When he visited Paris the last time, in 1744, M. de Fontenelle having remarked a slight Norman accent in his pronunciation, spoke of it to him, and asked him if he had not first been taught French by a person from Normandy, which turned out to be the case.

After two years of university life, he made his Continental tour, according to the custom of young Englishmen. He visited Holland, Italy, and France. He wrote from Paris to M. Jouneau on the 7th of December, 1714, as follows:

"I shall not tell you what I think of the French, because I am being often taken for a Frenchman, and more than one of them has paid me the highest possible compliment, by saying: '*Monsieur, you are quite one of ourselves.*' I shall only tell you that I am impudent; that I talk a great deal very loudly and with an air of authority; that I sing; that I dance in my walk; and, finally, that I spend immense sums in powder, feathers, white gloves, etc."

In this extract one recognizes the mocking, satirical, and slightly *insolent* wit, who makes his mark for the first time at the expense of the French; he will do justice later to our serious qualities. In his letters to his son, he has pictured himself the first day he made his *entrée* into good society, still covered with the rust of Cambridge, shamefaced, embarrassed, silent; and, finally, forcing his courage with both hands to say to a beautiful woman near him: "Madame, don't you find it very warm to-day?" But Lord Chesterfield told his son that to encourage him, and to show what it is necessary to pass through. He makes himself an example to embolden him, and to draw the boy more readily to him. I shall be careful not to take his word for this anecdote. If he was for a moment embarrassed in the world, the moment was assuredly very short, nor was he much concerned with it.

Immediately on the death of Queen Anne, Chesterfield hailed the accession of the house of Hanover, of which he became an avowed champion. He had at first a seat in the House of Commons, and made his *début* there with fair credit. But a circumstance, in appearance frivolous, kept him, it is said, in check, and in some measure paralyzed his eloquence. One of the members of the House, who was distinguished by no talent of a superior order, had that of imitating and counterfeiting to perfection the orators to whom he replied. Chesterfield was afraid of ridicule; it was one of his weaknesses, and he kept silence more than he otherwise would have done for fear of giving occasion for the exercise of his colleague and opponent's talent. He inherited a large property on the death of his father, and was raised to the Upper House, which was, perhaps, a better setting for the grace, finish, and urbanity of his eloquence. He found no comparison between the two scenes with regard to the importance of the debates and the political influence to be acquired.

"It is surprising," he said later of Pitt, at the time when that great orator consented to enter the Upper House as Lord Chatham, "it is surprising that a man in the plenitude of his power, at the very moment when his ambition has obtained the most complete triumph, should leave the House which procured him that power, and which alone could ensure its maintenance, to retire into that Hospital for Incurables, the House of Lords."

It is not my intention here to estimate the political career of Lord Chesterfield. Nevertheless, if I hazarded a judgment upon it as a whole, I should say that his ambition was never wholly satisfied, and that the brilliant distinctions with which his public life was filled, covered, at bottom, many lost desires and the decay of many hopes. Twice, in the two decisive circumstances of his political life, he failed. Young, and in the first heat of ambition, he took an early opportunity of staking his odds on the side of the heir presumptive to the throne, who became George the Second. He was one of those who, at the accession of that prince, counted most surely upon his favor, and upon enjoying a share of power. But this clever man, wishing to turn himself to the rising sun, knew not how to accomplish it with perfect justice; he had paid court to the prince's mistress, believing in her destined influence, and he had neglected the legitimate wife, the future queen, who alone had the real power. Queen Caroline never pardoned him, and this was the first check in the political fortune of Lord Chesterfield, then thirty-three years old, and in the full flush of hope. He was in too great a hurry and took the wrong road. Robert Walpole, less active, and with less apparent skill, took his measures and made his calculations better.

Thrown with *éclat* into the opposition, especially from 1732, the time when he had to cease his court duties, Lord Chesterfield worked with all his might for ten years for the downfall of Walpole, which did not take place until 1742. But even then he inherited none of his power, and he remained out of the new ministries. When two years afterward, in 1744, he became one of the administration, first as ambassador to The Hague and Viceroy of Ireland, then as Secretary of State and member of the Cabinet (1746-1748), the honor was more nominal than real. In a word, Lord Chesterfield, at all times a noted politician in his own country, whether as one of the chiefs of the opposition, or as a clever diplomatist, was never a powerful, or even a very influential, minister.

In politics he certainly possessed that far-sightedness and those glimpses into the future which belong to very wide intelligence, but he possessed those qualities to a much greater degree than the patient perseverance and constant practical firmness that are so necessary to the members of a government. It may truly be said of him, as of Rochefoucauld, that politics served to make an accomplished moralist of the imperfect man of action.

In 1744, when he was only fifty years of age, his political ambition, seemed, in part, to have died out, and the indifferent state of his health led him to choose a private life. And then the object of his secret ideal and his real ambition we know now. Before his marriage he had, about the year 1732, by a French lady (Madame de Bouchet) whom he met in Holland, a natural son to whom he was tenderly attached. He wrote to this son, in all sincerity: "From the first day of your life, the dearest object of mine has been to make you as perfect as the weakness of human nature will allow." Toward the education of this son all his wishes, all his affectionate and worldly predilections tended. And whether Viceroy of Ireland or Secretary of State in London, he found time to write long letters full of minute details to him, to instruct him in small matters and to perfect him in mind and manner.

The Chesterfield, then, that we love especially to study is the man of wit and experience, who knew all the affairs and passed through all phases of political and public life only to find out its smallest resources, and to tell us the last *mot*; he who from his youth was the friend of Pope and Bolingbroke, the introducer into England of Montesquieu and Voltaire, the correspondent of Fontenelle and Madame de Teucin, he whom the Academy of Inscriptions placed among its members, who united the wit of the two nations, and who, in more than one intellectual essay, but particularly in his letters to his son, shows himself to us as a moralist as amiable as he is consummate, and one of the masters of life. It is the Rochefoucauld of England of whom we speak. Montesquieu, after the publication of *L'Esprit des Lois*, wrote to the Abbé de Guasco, who was then in England: "Tell my Lord Chesterfield that nothing is so flattering to me as his approbation; but that, though he is reading my work for the third time, he will only be in a better position to point out to me what wants correcting and rectifying in it; nothing could be more instructive to me than his observations and his critique." It was Chesterfield who, speaking to Montesquieu one day of the readiness of the French for revolutions, and their impatience at slow reforms, spoke this sentence, which is a *résumé* of our whole history: "You French know how to make barricades, but you never raise barriers."

Lord Chesterfield certainly appreciated Voltaire; he remarked, *à propos* of the *Siècle de Louis XIV.*: "Lord Bolingbroke had taught me how to read history; Voltaire teaches me how it should be written." But, at the same time, with that practical sense which rarely abandons men of wit on the other side of the Straits, he felt the imprudences of Voltaire, and disapproved of them. When he was old, and living in retirement, he wrote to a French lady on the subject thus:

"Your good authors are my principal resource: Voltaire especially charms me, with the exception of his impiety, with which he cannot help seasoning all that he writes, and which he would do better carefully to suppress, for one ought not to disturb established order. Let every one think as he will, or rather as he can, but let him not communicate his ideas if they are of a nature to trouble the peace of society."

What he said then, in 1768, Chesterfield had already said more than twenty years previously, writing to the younger Crebillon, a singular correspondent and a singular confidant in point of morality. Voltaire was under consideration, on account of his tragedy of *Mahomet*, and the daring ideas it contains:

"What I do not pardon him for, and that which is not deserving of pardon in him," wrote Chesterfield to Crebillon, "is his desire to propagate a doctrine as pernicious to domestic society as contrary to the common religion of all countries. I strongly doubt whether it is permissible for a man to write against the worship and belief of his country, even if he be fully persuaded of its error, on account of the trouble and disorder it might cause; but I am sure that it is in no wise allowable to attack the foundations of true morality, and to break necessary bonds which are already too weak to keep men in the path of duty."

Chesterfield, in speaking thus, was not mistaken as to the great inconsistency of Voltaire. His inconsistency, in a few words, was this: Voltaire, who looked upon men as fools or children, and who could never laugh at them enough, at the same time put loaded firearms into their hands, without troubling himself as to the use they would put them to.

Lord Chesterfield himself, in the eyes of the Puritans of his country, has been accused, I should state here, of a breach of morality in the letters addressed to his son. The strict Johnson, who was not impartial on the subject, and who thought he had cause to complain against Chesterfield, said, when the letters were published, that "they taught the morals of a courtesan, and the manners of a dancing master."

Such a judgment is supremely unjust, and if Chesterfield, in particular instances, insists upon graces of manner at any price, it is because he has already provided for the more solid parts of education, and because his pupil is not in the least danger of sinning on the side which makes man *respectable*, but rather on that which renders him *agreeable*. Although more than one passage in these letters may seem very strange, coming from a father to a son, the whole is animated with a true spirit of tenderness and wisdom. If Horace had had a son, I imagine he would not have written to him very differently.

The letters begin with the A B C of education and instruction. Chesterfield teaches his son in French the rudiments of mythology and history. I do not regret the publication of these first letters. He lets slip some very excellent advice in those early pages. The little Stanhope is no more than eight years old when his father suits a little rhetoric to his juvenile understanding, and tries to show him how to use good language, and to express himself well. He especially recommends to him *attention* in all that he does, and he gives the word its full value. "It is attention alone," he says, "which fixes objects in the memory. There is no surer mark of a mean and meagre intellect in the world than inattention. All that is worth the trouble of doing at all deserves to be done well, and nothing can be well done without attention." This precept he incessantly repeats, and varies the application of it as his pupil grows, and is in a condition to comprehend it to its fullest extent. Whether pleasure or study, everything one does must be done well, done entirely and at its proper time, without allowing any distraction to intervene. "When you read Horace pay attention to the accuracy of his thoughts, to the elegance of his diction, and to the beauty of his poetry, and do not think of the '*De Homine et Cive*' of Puffendorf; and when you read Puffendorf do not think of Madame de St. Germain; nor of Puffendorf when you speak of Madame de St. Germain." But this strong and easy subjugation of the order of thought to the will only belongs to great or very good intellects. M. Royer-Collard used to say that "what was most wanting in our day was *respect* in the moral disposition, and *attention* in the intellectual." Lord Chesterfield, in a less grave manner, might have said the same thing. He was not long in finding out what was wanting in this child whom he wished to bring up; whose bringing up was, indeed, the end and aim of his life. "On sounding your character to its very depths," he said to him, "I have not, thank God, discovered any vice of heart or weakness of head so far; but I have discovered idleness, inattention, and indifference, defects which are only pardonable in the aged, who, in the decline of life, when health and spirits give way, have a sort of right to that kind of tranquillity. But a young man ought to be ambitious to shine and excel." And it is precisely this sacred fire, this lightning, that makes the Achilles, the Alexanders, and the Cæsars *to be the first in every undertaking*, this motto of noble hearts and of eminent men of all kinds, that nature had primarily neglected to place in the honest but thoroughly mediocre soul of the younger Stanhope: "You appear to want," said his father, "that *vivida vis animi* which excites the majority of young men to please, to strive, and to outdo others." "When I was your age," he again says, "I should have been ashamed for another to know his lesson better, or to have been before me in a game, and I should have had no rest till I had regained the advantage." All this little course of education by letters offers a sort of continuous dramatic interest; we follow the efforts of a fine distinguished, energetic nature as Lord Chesterfield's was, engaged in a contest with a disposition honest but indolent, with an easy and dilatory temperament, from which it would, at any expense, form a masterpiece accomplished, amiable and original, and with which it only succeeded in making a sort of estimable copy. What sustains and almost touches the reader in this strife, where so much art is used, and where the inevitable counsel is the same beneath all metamorphoses, is the true fatherly affection which animates and inspires the delicate and excellent master, as patient as he is full of vigor, lavish in resources and skill, never discouraged, untiring in sowing elegances and graces on this infantile soil. Not that this son, the object of so much culture and zeal, was in any way unworthy of his father. It has been pretended that there could be no one duller or more sullen than he was, and Johnson is quoted in support of the statement. There are caricatures which surpass the truth. It appears from the best authorities, that Mr. Stanhope, without being a model of grace, had the air of a man who had been well brought up, and was polite and agreeable. But do you not think that that is the most grievous part of all? It would have been better worth while, almost, to have totally failed, and to have only succeeded in making an original in the inverse sense, rather than with so much care and expense to have produced nothing more than an ordinary and insignificant man of the world, one of those about whom it suffices to say, there is nothing to be said of them; he had cause to be truly grieved and pity himself for his work if he were not a father.

Lord Chesterfield had early thought of France to polish his son, and to give him that courtesy which cannot be acquired late in life. In private letters written to a lady at Paris, whom I believe to be Madame de Monconseil,14 we see that he had thought of sending him to France from his childhood.

"I have a boy," he wrote to this friend, "who is now thirteen years old; I freely confess to you that he is not legitimate; but his mother was well born and was kinder to me than I deserved. As to the boy, perhaps it is partiality, but I think him amiable; he has a pretty face; he has much sprightliness, and I think intelligence, for his age. He speaks French perfectly; he knows a good deal of Latin and Greek, and he has ancient and modern history at his fingers' ends. He is at school at present, but as they never dream of forming the manners of young people, and they are almost all foolish, awkward, and unpolished, in short such as you see them when they come to Paris at the age of twenty or twenty-one, I do not wish my boy to remain here to acquire such bad habits; for this reason, when he is fourteen I think of sending him to Paris. As I love the child dearly, and have set myself to make something good of him, as I believe he has the stuff in him, my idea is to unite in him what has never been found in one person before—I mean the best qualities of the two nations."

And he enters into the details of his plan, and the means he thinks of using: a learned Englishman every morning, a French teacher after dinner, but above all the help of the fashionable world and good society. The war which broke out between France and England postponed this plan, and the young man did not make his *début* in Paris until 1751, when he was nineteen years old, and had finished his tour through Switzerland, Germany, and Italy.

Everything has been arranged by the most attentive of fathers for his success and well-being upon this novel scene. The young man is placed at the Academy with M. de la Guérinière; the morning he devotes to study, and the rest of the time is to be consecrated to the world. "Pleasure is now the last branch of your education," this indulgent father writes; "it will soften and polish your manners; it will incite you to seek and finally to acquire *graces*." Upon this last point he is exacting, and shows no quarter. *Graces*, he returns continually to them, for without them all effort is vain. "If they are not natural to you, cultivate them," he cries. He indeed speaks confidently; as if to cultivate graces, it is not necessary to have them already!

Three ladies, friends of his father, are especially charged to watch over and guide the young man at his *début*; they are his *governantes*: Madame de Monconseil, Lady Hervey, and Madame de Bocage. But these introducers appear essential for the first time only; the young man must afterward depend upon himself, and choose some charming and more familiar guide. Upon this delicate subject of women, Lord Chesterfield breaks the ice: "I shall not talk to you on this subject like a theologian, or a moralist, or a father," he says; "I set aside my age, and only take yours into consideration. I wish to speak to you as one man of pleasure would to another if he has taste and spirit." And he expresses himself in consequence, stimulating the young man as much as possible toward *polite arrangements* and delicate pleasures, to draw him from common and coarse habits. His principle is that "a polite arrangement becomes a gallant man." All his morality on this point is summed up in a line of Voltaire:

"Il n'est jamais de mal en bonne compagnie."

It is at these sentences more especially that the modesty of the grave Johnson is put to the blush; ours is content to smile at them.

The serious and the frivolous are perpetually mingling in these letters. Marcel, the dancing master, is very often recommended, Montesquieu no less. The Abbé de Guasco, a sort of toady to Montesquieu, is a useful personage for introductions. "Between you and me," writes Chesterfield, "he has more knowledge than genius; but *a clever man knows how to make use of everything*, and every man is good for something. As to the Président of Montesquieu, he is in all respects a precious acquaintance: *He has genius, with the most extensive reading in the world. Drink of his fountain as much as possible.*"

Of authors, those whom Chesterfield particularly recommends at this time, and those whose names occur most frequently in his counsels, are La Rochefoucauld and La Bruyère. "If you read some of La Rochefoucauld's maxims in the morning, consider them, examine them well, and compare them with the originals you meet in the evening. Read La Bruyère in the morning, and see in the evening if his portraits are correct." But these guides, excellent as they are, have no other use by themselves than that of a map. Without personal observation and experience, they would be useless, and would even be conducive to error, as a map might be if one thought to get from it a complete knowledge of towns and provinces. Better read one man than ten books. "The world is a country that no one has ever known by means of descriptions; each of us must traverse it in person to be thoroughly initiated into its ways."

Here are some precepts or remarks which are worthy of those masters of human morality:

"The most essential of all knowledge, I mean the knowledge of the world, is never acquired without great attention, and I know a great many aged persons who, after having had an extensive acquaintance, are still mere children in the knowledge of the world."

"Human nature is the same all over the world; but its operations are so varied by education and custom that we ought to see it in all its aspects to get an intimate knowledge of it."

"Almost all men are born with every passion to some extent, but there is hardly a man who has not a dominant passion to which the others are subordinate. Discover this governing passion in every individual; search into the recesses of his heart, and observe the different effects of the same passion in different people. And when you have found the master passion of a man, remember never to trust to him where that passion is concerned."

"If you wish particularly to gain the good graces and affection of certain people, men or women, try to discover their most striking merit, if they have one, and their dominant weakness, for every one has his own, then do justice to the one, and *a little more than justice to the other.*"

"Women, in general, have only one object, which is their beauty, upon which subject hardly any flattery can be too gross to please them."

"The flattery which is most pleasing to really beautiful or decidedly ugly women, is that which is addressed to their intellect."

On the subject of women, again, if he seems disdainful now and then, he makes reparation elsewhere; and, above all, whatever he thinks of them, he never allows his son to slander them too much. "You appear to think that from the days of *Eve* to the present time they have done much harm: as regards *that lady* I agree with you; but from her time history teaches you that men have done more harm in the world than women; and to speak truly, I would warn you not to trust either sex more than is absolutely necessary. But what I particularly advise you is this: never to attack whole bodies, whatever they may be."

"Individuals occasionally forgive, but bodies and societies never do."

In general, Chesterfield counsels his son to be circumspect and to preserve a sort of prudent neutrality, even in the case of the knaves and fools with which the world abounds. "After their friendship there is nothing more dangerous than to have them for enemies." It is not the morality of Cato nor of Zeno, but that of Alcibiades, of Aristippus, or Atticus.

Upon religion he shall speak, in reply to some trenchant opinion that his son had expressed: "The reason of every man is and ought to be his guide; and I shall have as much right to expect every man to be of my height and temperament, as to wish that he should reason precisely as I do."

In everything he is of the opinion that the good and the best should be known and loved, but that it is not necessary to make one's self a champion for or against everything. One must know even in literature how to tolerate the weaknesses of others: "Let them enjoy quietly their errors both in taste and religion." Oh! how far from such wisdom is the bitter trade of criticism, as we do it!

He does not, however, advise lying; he is precise in this particular. His precept always runs thus: do not tell all, but never tell a lie. "I have always observed," he frequently repeats, "that the greatest fools are the greatest liars. For my part, I judge of the truth of a man by the extent of his intellect."

We see how really he mixes the useful and the agreeable. He is perpetually demanding from the intellect something resolute and subtle, sweetness in the manner, energy at bottom.

Lord Chesterfield thoroughly appreciated the serious state of France and the dread events that the eighteenth century brought to light. According to him, Duclos, in his *Reflections*, is right when he says that "*a germ of reason is beginning to appear in France.*" "What I can confidently predict," adds Chesterfield, "is that before the end of this century the trades of king and priest will have lost half their power."

Our revolution has been clearly predicted by him since 1750.

He warned his son from the beginning against the idea that the French are entirely frivolous. "The cold inhabitants of the north look upon the French as a frivolous people who sing and whistle and dance perpetually; this is very far from being the truth, though the army of *fops* seems to justify it. But these *fops*, ripened by age and experience, often turn into very able men." The ideal, according to him, would be to unite the merits of the two nations; but in this mixture he still seems to lean toward France: "I have said many times, and I really think, that a Frenchman who joins to a good foundation of virtue, learning, and good sense, the manners and politeness of his country, has attained the perfection of human nature." He unites sufficiently well in himself the advantages of the two nations, with one characteristic which belongs exclusively to his race—there is imagination even in his wit. Hamilton himself has this distinctive characteristic, and introduces it into French wit. Bacon, the great moralist, is almost a poet by expression. One cannot say so much of Lord Chesterfield; nevertheless, he has more imagination in his sallies and in the expression of his wit than one meets with in Saint Evremond and our acute moralists in general. He resembles his friend Montesquieu in this respect.

If in the letters to his son we can, without being severe, lay hold of some cases of slightly damaged morality, we should have to point out, by way of compensation, some very serious and really admirable passages, where he speaks of the Cardinal de Retz, of Mazarin, of Bolingbroke, of Marlborough, and of many others. It is a rich book. One cannot read a page without finding some happy observation worthy of being remembered.

Lord Chesterfield intended this beloved son for a diplomatic life; he at first found some difficulties in the way on account of his illegitimacy. To cut short these objections, he sent his son to Parliament; it was the surest method of conquering the scruples of the court. Mr. Stanhope, in his maiden speech, hesitated a moment, and was obliged to have recourse to notes. He did not make a second attempt at speaking in public. It appears that he succeeded better in diplomacy, in those second-rate places where solid merit is sufficient. He filled the post of ambassador extraordinary to the court of Dresden. But his health, always delicate, failed before he was old, and his father had the misfortune to see him die before him when he was scarcely thirty-six years old (1768). Lord Chesterfield at that time lived entirely retired from the world, on account of his infirmities, the most painful of which was complete deafness. Montesquieu, whose sight failed, said to him once, "*I know how to be blind.*" But he was not able to say as much; he did not know how to be deaf. He wrote of it to his friends, even to those in France, thus: "The exchange of letters," he remarked, "is the conversation of deaf people, and the only link which connects them with society." He found his latest consolations in his pretty country-house at Blackheath, which he had called by the French name of Babiole. He employed his time there in gardening and cultivating his melons and pineapples; he amused himself by vegetating *in company with them.*

"I have vegetated here all this year," he wrote to a French friend (September, 1753), "without pleasures and without troubles; my age and deafness prevented the first; my philosophy, or rather my temperament (for one often confounds them), guaranteed me against the last. I always get as much as I can of the quiet pleasures of gardening, walking, and reading, and in the meantime *I await death without desiring or fearing it.*"

He never undertook long works, not feeling himself sufficiently strong, but he sometimes sent agreeable essays to a periodical publication, *The World.* These essays are quite worthy of his reputation for skill and urbanity. Nevertheless, nothing approaches the work — which was no work to him — of those letters, which he never imagined any one would read, and which are yet the foundation of his literary success.

His old age, which was an early one, lasted a long time. His wit gave a hundred turns to this sad theme. Speaking of himself and one of his friends, Lord Tyrawley, equally old and infirm: "Tyrawley and I," he said, "have been dead two years, but we do not wish it to be known."

Voltaire, who under the pretence of being always dying, had preserved his youth much better, wrote to him on the 24th of October, 1771, this pretty letter, signed "*Le vieux malade de Ferney*":

"Enjoy an honorable and happy old age, after having passed through the trials of life. Enjoy your wit and preserve the health of your body. Of the five senses with which we are provided, you have only one enfeebled, and Lord Huntingdon assures me that you have a good stomach, which is worth a pair of ears. It will be perhaps my place to decide which is the most sorrowful, to be deaf or blind, or have no digestion. I can judge of all these three conditions with a knowledge of the cause; but it is a long time since I ventured to decide upon trifles, least of all upon things so important. I confine myself to the belief that, if you have sun in the beautiful house that you have built, you will spend some tolerable moments; that is all we can hope for at our age. Cicero wrote a beautiful treatise upon old age, but he did not verify his words by deeds; his last years were very unhappy. You have lived longer and more happily than he did. You have had to do neither with perpetual dictators nor with triumvirs. Your lot has been, and still is, one of the most desirable in that great lottery where good tickets are so scarce, and where the Great Prize of continual happiness has never been gained by any one. Your philosophy has never been upset by chimeras which have sometimes perplexed tolerably good brains. *You have never been in any sense a charlatan, nor the dupe of charlatans*, and that I reckon as a rare merit, which adds something to the shadow of happiness that we are allowed to taste of in this short life."

Lord Chesterfield died on the 24th of March, 1773. In pointing out his charming course of worldly education, we have not thought it out of place even in a Democracy,15 to take lessons of *savoir vivre* and politeness, and to receive them from a man whose name is so closely connected with those of Montesquieu and Voltaire, who, more than any other of his countrymen in his own time, showed singular fondness for our nation; who delighted, more than was right, perhaps, in our amiable qualities; who appreciated our solid virtues, and of whom it might be said, as his greatest praise, that he was a French wit, if he had not introduced into the *verve* and vivacity of his sallies that inexplicable something of imagination and color that bears the impress of his race.

LORD CHESTERFIELD'S LETTERS, SENTENCES, AND MAXIMS.

Travel in Holland.—On me dit, Monsieur! que vous vous disposez à voyager, et que vous débutez par la Hollande. De sorte j'ai crû de mon devoir, de vous souhaiter un bon voyage, et des vents favorables. Vous aurez la bonté, j'espère, de me faire part de votre arrivée à la Haye; et si après cela, dans le cours de vos voyages, vous faites quelques remarques curieuses, vous voudrez bien me les communiquer.

La Hollande, où vous allez, est de beaucoup la plus belle, et la plus riche des Sept Provinces-Unies, qui, toutes ensemble, forment la République. Les autres sont celles de Gueldres, Zélande, Frise, Utrecht, Groningue, et Over-Yssel. Les Sept Provinces composent, ce qu'on appelle les Etats Généraux des Provinces-Unies, et font une République très-puissante, et très-considérable.16

Translation.—I am informed, sir, that you are about to travel, and that you will start with Holland. Therefore I have thought it my duty to wish you a pleasant journey and favorable winds. You will, I am sure, be so good as to acquaint me with your arrival at The Hague; and afterward, if in your travels you should observe anything curious, will you let me know?

Holland, where you are going, is by far the finest and richest of the seven united provinces, which together form the Republic. The other provinces are Guelderland, Zealand, Friesland, Utrecht, Groningen, and Overyssel; these seven provinces form what is called the States-General of the United Provinces, etc.17

True Decency.—One of the most important points of life is decency; which is to do what is proper, and where it is proper; for many things are proper at one time, and in one place, that are extremely improper in another; for example, it is very proper and decent that you should play some part of the day; but you must feel that it would be very improper and indecent if you were to fly your kite, or play at nine-pins while you are with Mr. Maittaire.18 It is very proper and decent to dance well; but then you must dance only at balls and places of entertainment; for you would be reckoned a fool if you were to dance at church or at a funeral. I hope, by these examples, you understand the meaning of the word *decency*, which in French is *bienséance*; in Latin, *decorum*; and in Greek, πρέπον. Cicero says of it, *Sic hoc decorum quod elucet in vitâ, movet approbationem earum quibuscum vivatur, ordine et constantiâ, et moderatione dictorum omnium atque factorum*: by which you see how necessary decency is to gain the approbation of mankind. And, as I am sure you desire to gain Mr. Maittaire's approbation, without which you will never have mine, I dare say you will mind and give attention to whatever he says to you, and behave yourself seriously and decently while you are with him; afterward play, run, and jump as much as ever you please. [*July 24, 1739.*]

The Art of Speaking. — You cannot but be convinced that a man who speaks and writes with elegance and grace; who makes choice of good words, and adorns and embellishes the subject upon which he either speaks or writes, will persuade better, and succeed more easily in obtaining what he wishes, than a man who does not explain himself clearly; speaks his language ill; or makes use of low and vulgar expressions; and who has neither grace nor elegance in anything that he says. Now it is by rhetoric that the art of speaking eloquently is taught; and, though I cannot think of grounding you in it as yet, I would wish, however, to give you an idea of it suitable to your age.19

The first thing you should attend to is, to speak whatever language you do speak, in its greatest purity, and according to the rules of grammar; for we must never offend against grammar, nor make use of words which are not really words. This is not all; for not to speak ill, is not sufficient; we must speak well; and the best method of attaining to that, is to read the best authors with attention; and to observe how people of fashion speak, and those who express themselves best; for shopkeepers, common people, footmen, and maid-servants all speak ill. [*Bath, Oct. 17, 1739.*]

Oratory. — The business of oratory is to persuade people; and you easily feel that to please people is a great step toward persuading them. You must, then, consequently, be sensible how advantageous it is for a man, who speaks in public, whether it be in Parliament, in the pulpit, or at the bar (that is, in the courts of law), to please his hearers so much as to gain their attention: which he can never do without the help of oratory. It is not enough to speak the language he speaks in its utmost purity, and according to the rules of grammar; but he must speak it elegantly; that is, he must choose the best and most expressive words, and put them in the best order. He should likewise adorn what he says by proper metaphors, similes, and other figures of rhetoric; and he should enliven it, if he can, by quick and sprightly turns of wit. [*November, 1739.*]

The Folly of Ignorance. — An ignorant man is insignificant and contemptible; nobody cares for his company, and he can just be said to live, and that is all. There is a very pretty French epigram upon the death of such an ignorant, insignificant fellow, the sting of which is, that all that can be said of him is, that he was once alive, and that he is now dead. This is the epigram, which you may get by heart:

"Colas est mort de maladie,

Tu veux que j'en pleure le sort,

Que diable veux-tu que j'en dis?

Colas vivoit. Colas est mort."

Take care not to deserve the name of Colas,20 which I shall certainly give you, if you do not learn well. [*No date.*]

Philippus Chesterfield parvulo suo Philippo Stanhope, S. P. D.

Pergrata mihi fuit epistola tua, quam nuper accepi, eleganter enim scripta erat, et polliceris te summam operam daturum, ut veras laudes meritò adipisci possis. Sed ut planè dicam; valde suspicor te, in ea scribenda, optimum et eruditissimum adjutorem habuisse; quo duce et auspice, nec elegantia, nec doctrina, nec quicquid prorsus est dignum sapiente bonoque, unquam tibi deesse poterit. Illum ergo ut quam diligenter colas, te etiam atque etiam rogo; et quo magis eum omni officio, amore, et obsequio persequeris, eo magis te me studiosum, et observantem existimabo.21

A Study in Verse. — To use your ear a little to English verse, and to make you attend to the sense, too, I have transposed the words of the following lines; which I would have you put in their proper order, and send me in your next:

"Life consider cheat a when 'tis all I

Hope the fool'd deceit men yet with favor

Repay will to-morrow trust on think and

Falser former day to-morrow's than the

Worse lies blest be shall when and we says it

Hope new some possess'd cuts off with we what."

[This is curious, and truly no bad way of teaching a child the structure of verse. The citation, a fine one, is from Dryden:

"When I consider life, 'tis all a cheat,

Yet fool'd with hope men favor the deceit."

The reader may puzzle out the rest.]

Virtue Discouraged. — If six hundred citizens of Athens gave in the name of any one Athenian, written upon an oyster-shell (from whence it is called ostracism), that man was banished Athens for ten years. On one hand, it is certain, that a free people cannot be too careful or jealous of their liberty; and it is certain, too, that the love and applause of mankind will always attend a man of eminent and distinguished virtue; and, consequently, they are more likely to give up their liberties to such-a-one than to another of less merit. But then, on the other hand, it seems extraordinary to discourage virtue upon any account; since it is only by virtue that any society can flourish, and be considerable. There are many more arguments, on each side of this question, which will naturally occur to you; and when you have considered them well, I desire you will write me your opinion, whether the ostracism was a right or a wrong thing, and your reasons for being of that opinion. Let nobody help you, and give me exactly your own sentiments and your own reasons, whatever they are. [*October, 1740.*]

Ambition. — Everybody has ambition of some kind or other, and is vexed when that ambition is disappointed; the difference is, that the ambition of silly people is a silly and mistaken ambition; and the ambition of people of sense is a right and commendable one. For instance, the ambition of a silly boy, of your age, would be to have fine clothes, and money to throw away in idle follies; which, you plainly see, would be no proofs of merit in him, but only of folly in his parents, in dressing him out like a jackanapes, and giving him money to play the fool with. Whereas a boy of good sense places his ambition in excelling other boys of his own age, and even older, in virtue and knowledge. His glory is in being known always to speak the truth, in showing good nature and compassion, in learning quicker, and applying himself more than other boys. These are real proofs of merit in him, and consequently proper objects of ambition; and will acquire him a solid reputation and character. This holds true in men as well as in boys; the ambition of a silly fellow will be to have a fine equipage, a fine house, and fine clothes; things which anybody, that has as much money, may have as well as he; *for they are all to be bought*; but the ambition of a man of sense and honor is to be distinguished by a character and reputation of knowledge, truth, and virtue — things which are not to be bought, and that can only be acquired by a good head and a good heart. [*Not dated.*]

Humanity. — It is certain that humanity is the particular *characteristic* of a great mind; little, vicious minds are full of anger and revenge, and are incapable of feeling the *exalted* pleasure of forgiving their enemies, and of bestowing marks of favor and generosity upon those of whom they have gotten the better. Adieu!22

Novels and Romances. — A novel is a kind of abbreviation of a romance; for a romance generally consists of twelve volumes, all filled with insipid love nonsense, and most incredible adventures. The subject of a romance is sometimes a story entirely fictitious, that is to say, quite invented; at other times a true story, but generally so changed and altered that one cannot know it. For example: in "Grand Cyrus," "Clelia," and "Cleopatra," three celebrated romances, there is some true history; but so blended with falsities and silly love adventures, that they confuse and corrupt the mind, instead of forming and instructing it. The greatest heroes of antiquity are there represented in woods and forests, whining insipid love tales to their inhuman fair one; who answers them in the same style. In short, the reading of romances is a most frivolous occupation, and time merely thrown away. [The little boy was then reading the historical novel of "Don Carlos," by the Abbé de St. Real. (*Not dated.*)]

Virtue.—Virtue is a subject that deserves your and every man's attention; and suppose I were to bid you make some verses, or give me your thoughts in prose, upon the subject of virtue, how would you go about it? Why, you would first consider what virtue is, and then what are the effects and marks of it, both with regard to others and one's self. You would find, then, that virtue consists in doing good, and in speaking truth; and that the effects of it are advantageous to all mankind, and to one's self in particular. Virtue makes us pity and relieve the misfortunes of mankind; it makes us promote justice and good order in society; and, in general, contributes to whatever tends to the real good of mankind. To ourselves it gives an inward comfort and satisfaction which nothing else can do, and which nothing can rob us of. All other advantages depend upon others, as much as upon ourselves. Riches, power, and greatness may be taken away from us by the violence and injustice of others or inevitable accidents, but virtue depends only on ourselves and nobody can take it away. [*Headed only Sunday.*]

The Reward of Virtue.—If a virtuous man be ever so poor or unfortunate in the world, still his virtue is his own reward and will comfort him under his afflictions. The quiet and satisfaction of his conscience make him cheerful by day and sleep sound of nights; he can be alone with pleasure and is not afraid of his own thoughts. Besides this, he is esteemed and respected; for even the most wicked people themselves cannot help admiring and respecting virtue in others. A poet says:

"Ipsa quidem virtus, sibimet pulcherrima merces."23

Politeness a Necessity.—Know, then, that as learning, honor, and virtue are absolutely necessary to gain you the esteem and admiration of mankind; politeness and good breeding are equally necessary, to make you welcome and agreeable in conversation and common life. Great talents, such as honor, virtue, learning, and parts, are above the generality of the world; who neither possess them themselves, nor judge of them rightly in others; but all people are judges of the lesser talents, such as civility, affability, and an obliging, agreeable address and manner; because they feel the good effects of them, as making society easy and pleasing.

Good Breeding and Good Sense.—Good sense must, in many cases, determine good breeding; because the same thing that would be civil at one time, and to one person, may be quite otherwise at another time, and to another person; but there are some general rules of good breeding, that hold always true, and in all cases. [*About February, 1741.*]

Rudeness and Civility.—I dare say I need not tell you how rude it is, to take the best place in a room, or to seize immediately upon what you like at table, without offering first to help others; as if you consider nobody but yourself. On the contrary, you should always endeavor to procure all the conveniences you can to the people you are with. Besides being civil, which is absolutely necessary, the perfection of good breeding is, to be civil with ease, and in a gentlemanlike manner. For this, you should observe the French people; who excel in it, and whose politeness seems as easy and natural as any other part of their conversation. Whereas the English are often awkward in their civilities, and, when they mean to be civil, are too much ashamed to get it out.

Mauvaise Honte.—Pray, do you remember never to be ashamed of doing what is right; you would have a great deal of reason to be ashamed, if you were not civil; but what reason can you have to be ashamed of being civil? And why not say a civil and an obliging thing, as easily and as naturally, as you would ask what o'clock it is? This kind of bashfulness, which is justly called, by the French, *mauvaise honte*, is the distinguishing character of an English booby; who is frightened out of his wits when people of fashion speak to him; and when he is to answer them, blushes, stammers, can hardly get out what he would say, and becomes really ridiculous, from a groundless fear of being laughed at; whereas a well bred man would speak to all the kings in the world with as little concern and as much ease as he would speak to you.

Youthful Emulation.—This is the last letter I shall write to you as to a little boy; for, to-morrow, if I am not mistaken, you will attain your ninth year; so that for the future I shall treat you as a *youth*. You must now commence a different course of life, a different course of studies. No more levity; childish toys and playthings must be thrown aside, and your mind directed to serious objects. What was not unbecoming of a child would be disgraceful to a youth. Wherefore, endeavor, with all your might, to show a suitable change; and, by learning, good manners, politeness, and other accomplishments, to surpass those youths of your own age, whom hitherto you have surpassed when boys.24 May the Almighty preserve you and bestow on you his choicest blessings.

True Respect. — The strictest and most scrupulous honor and virtue can alone make you esteemed and valued by mankind; [remember] that parts and learning can alone make you admired and celebrated by them; but that the possession of lesser talents is most absolutely necessary, toward making you liked, beloved, and sought after in private life. Of these lesser talents, good breeding is the principal and most necessary one, not only as it is very important itself; but as it adds great lustre to the more solid advantages both of the heart and the mind.

Manner. — An easy manner and carriage must be wholly free from those odd tricks, ill habits, and awkwardnesses, which even very worthy and sensible people have in their behavior. [*May, 1741.*]

Manner — Absence — Awkwardness — Attention. — However trifling a genteel manner may sound, it is of very great consequence towards pleasing in private life, especially the women; which (*sic*), one time or other, you will think worth pleasing; and I have known many a man, from his awkwardness, give people such a dislike of him at first, that all his merit could not get the better of it afterwards. Whereas a genteel manner prepossesses people in your favor, bends them towards you and makes them wish to like you. Awkwardness can proceed but from two causes: either from not having kept good company, or from not having attended to it. As for your keeping good company, I will take care of that; do you take care to observe their ways and manners, and to form your own upon them. Attention is absolutely necessary for this, as, indeed, it is for everything else; and a man without attention is not fit to live in the world. When an awkward fellow first comes into a room it is highly probable that his sword gets between his legs, and throws him down, or makes him stumble at least; when he has recovered this accident, he goes and places himself in the very place of the whole room where he should not; there he soon lets his hat fall down, and, in taking it up again, throws down his cane; in recovering his cane, his hat falls a second time; so that he is a quarter of an hour before he is in order again. If he drinks tea or coffee, he certainly scalds his mouth, and lets either the cup or the saucer fall, and spills the tea or coffee in his breeches. At dinner his awkwardness distinguishes itself particularly, as he has more to do; there he holds his knife, fork, and spoon differently from other people; eats with his knife to the great danger of his mouth, picks his teeth with his fork, and puts his spoon, which has been in his throat twenty times, into the dishes again. If he is to carve, he can never hit the joint; but, in his vain efforts to cut through the bone, scatters the sauce in everybody's face. He generally daubs himself with soup and grease, though his napkin is commonly stuck through a buttonhole, and tickles his chin. When he drinks, he infallibly coughs in his glass and besprinkles the company. Besides all this, he has strange tricks and gestures; such as snuffing up his nose, making faces, putting his fingers in his nose, or blowing it and looking afterward in his handkerchief, so as to make the company sick. His hands are troublesome to him when he has not something in them, and he does not know where to put them; but they are in perpetual motion between his bosom and his breeches; he does not wear his clothes, and, in short, does nothing like other people. All this, I own, is not in any degree criminal; but it is highly disagreeable and ridiculous in company, and ought most carefully to be avoided by whoever desires to please.

From this account of what you should not do, you may easily judge what you should do; and a due attention to the manners of people of fashion, and who have seen the world, will make it habitual and familiar to you.

There is, likewise, an awkwardness of expression and words, most carefully to be avoided; such as false English, bad pronunciation, old sayings, and common proverbs; which are so many proofs of having kept bad and low company. For example: if, instead of saying that tastes are different, and that every man has his own peculiar one, you should let off a proverb, and say, "What is one man's meat is another man's poison"; or else, "Every one as they like, as the good man said when he kissed his cow"; everybody would be persuaded that you had never kept company with anybody above footmen and housemaids.

Attention will do all this; and without attention nothing is to be done; want of attention, which is really want of thought, is either folly or madness. You should not only have attention to everything, but a quickness of attention, so as to observe, at once, all the people in the room; their motions, their looks, and their words; and yet without staring at them, and seeming to be an observer. This quick and unobserved observation is of infinite advantage in life, and is to be acquired with care; and, on the contrary, what is called absence, which is a thoughtlessness and want of attention about what is doing, makes a man so like either a fool or a madman, that, for my part, I see no real difference. A fool never has thought, a madman has lost it; and an absent man is, for the time, without it.25 [*Dated Spa, July 25, N. S. 1741.*]

True Praise. — *Laudari a viro laudato* was always a commendable ambition; encourage that ambition and continue to deserve the praises of the praiseworthy. While you do so you shall have everything you will from me; and when you cease to do so you shall have nothing.

An Awkward Mind. — I have warned you against odd motions, strange postures, and ungenteel carriage. But there is likewise an awkwardness of the mind that ought to be, and with care may be, avoided; as, for instance, to mistake or forget names; to speak of Mr. What-d'ye-call-him, or Mrs. Thingum, or How-d'ye-call-her, is excessively awkward and ordinary. To call people by improper titles and appellations is so, too; as my Lord for sir; and sir for my Lord. To begin a story or narration, when you are not perfect in it, and cannot go through with it, but are forced, possibly, to say in the middle of it, "I have forgot the rest," is very unpleasant and bungling. One must be extremely exact, clear, and perspicuous in everything one says, otherwise, instead of entertaining or informing others, one only tires and puzzles them. The voice and manner of speaking, too, are not to be neglected; some people almost shut their mouths when they speak, and mutter so, that they are not to be understood; others speak so fast and sputter so, that they are not to be understood neither; some always speak as loud as if they were talking to deaf people; and others so low that one cannot hear them. All these habits are awkward and disagreeable; and are to be avoided by attention; they are the distinguishing marks of the ordinary people, who have had no care taken of their education. You cannot imagine how necessary it is to mind all these little things; for I have seen many people with great talents ill received, for want of having these talents, too; and others well received only from their little talents, and who had no great ones.

Oratory and Hard Work. — Demosthenes, the celebrated Greek orator, thought it so absolutely necessary to speak well, that though he naturally stuttered, and had weak lungs, he resolved, by application and care, to get the better of those disadvantages. Accordingly, he cured his stammering by putting small pebbles into his mouth; and strengthened his lungs gradually, by using himself every day to speak aloud and distinctly for a considerable time. He likewise went often to the seashore, in stormy weather, when the sea made most noise, and there spoke as loud as he could, in order to use himself to the noise and murmurs of the popular assemblies of the Athenians, before whom he was to speak. By such care, joined to the constant study of the best authors, he became at last the greatest orator of his own or any other age or country, though he was born without any one natural talent for it. Adieu! Copy Demosthenes. [(?) *August, 1741.*]

Keep your Word. — I am sure you know that breaking of your word is a folly, a dishonor, and a crime. It is a folly, because nobody will trust you afterward; and it is both a dishonor and a crime, truth being the first duty of religion and morality; and whoever has not truth cannot be supposed to have any one good quality, and must become the detestation of God and man. Therefore I expect, from your truth and your honor, that you will do that, which independently of your promise, your own interest and ambition ought to incline you to do; that is, to excel in everything you undertake. When I was of your age, I should have been ashamed if any boy of that age had learned his book better, or played at any play better than I did; and I would not have rested a moment till I had got before him. Julius Cæsar, who had a noble thirst of glory, used to say that he would rather be the first in a village than the second in Rome; and he even cried when he saw the statue of Alexander the Great, with the reflection of how much more glory Alexander had acquired, at thirty years old, than he at a much more advanced age. These are the sentiments to make people considerable; and those who have them not will pass their lives in obscurity and contempt; whereas those who endeavor to excel all, are at least sure of excelling a great many. [*June, 1742.*]

Good Breeding. — Though I need not tell one of your age,26 experience, and knowledge of the world, how necessary good breeding is, to recommend one to mankind; yet, as your various occupations of Greek and cricket, Latin and pitch-farthing, may possibly divert your attention from this object, I take the liberty of reminding you of it, and desiring you to be very well bred at Lord Orrery's. It is good breeding alone that can prepossess people in your favor at first sight; more time being necessary to discover greater talents. This good breeding, you know, does not consist in low bows and formal ceremony; but in an easy, civil, and respectful behavior. You will therefore take care to answer with complaisance, when you are spoken to; to place yourself at the lower end of the table, unless bid to go higher; to drink first to the lady of the house, and next to the master; not to eat awkwardly or dirtily; not to sit when others stand; and to do all this with an air of complaisance, and not with a grave, sour look, as if you did it at all unwillingly. [*No date, Letter 70.*]

Letter Writing. — Let your letter be written as accurately as you are able — I mean with regard to language, grammar, and stops; for as to the *matter* of it the less trouble you give yourself the better it will be. Letters should be easy and natural, and convey to the persons to whom we send them, just what we should say to the persons if we were with them. [*No date, Letter 72.*]

The Results of Carelessness. — To this oscitancy we owe so many mistakes, hiatus's (*sic*), lacunæ, etc., in ancient manuscripts. It may be here necessary to explain to you the meaning of the *oscitantes librarii*; which I believe you will easily take. These persons (before printing was invented) transcribed the works of authors, sometimes for their own profit, but oftener (as they were generally slaves) for the profit of their masters. In the first case, dispatch, more than accuracy, was their object; for the faster they wrote the more they got; in the latter case (observe this), as it was a task imposed on them, which they did not dare to refuse, they were *idle, careless, and incorrect; not giving themselves the trouble to read over what they had written.*

The celebrated Atticus kept a great number of these transcribing slaves, and got great sums of money by their labors. [*November, 1745.*]

Greek Epigrams.—I hope you will keep company with Horace and Cicero among the Romans; and Homer and Xenophon among the Greeks, and that you have got out of the worst company in the world, the Greek epigrams. Martial has wit and is worth your looking into sometimes, but I recommend the Greek epigrams to your supreme contempt. Good-night to you. [*Same date.*]

Dancing Trifling.—Dancing is in itself a very trifling, silly thing; but it is one of those established follies to which people of sense are sometimes obliged to conform; and then they should be able to do it well. And, though I would not have you a dancer, yet, when you do dance, I would have you dance well, as I would have you do everything you do, well. There is no one thing so trifling, but which (if it is to be done at all) ought to be done well. And I have often told you that I wished you even played at pitch and cricket better than any boy at Westminster. For instance: dress is a very foolish thing; and yet it is a very foolish thing for a man not to be well dressed, according to his rank and way of life; and it is so far from being a disparagement to any man's understanding, that it is rather a proof of it, to be as well dressed as those whom he lives with. The difference in this case between a man of sense and a fop is, that the fop values himself upon his dress; and the man of sense laughs at it, at the same time that he knows he must not neglect it. There are a thousand foolish customs of this kind, which not being criminal must be complied with, and even cheerfully, by men of sense. Diogenes the cynic was a wise man for despising them, but a fool for showing it. Be wiser than other people if you can, but do not tell them so. [*Dublin Castle, Nov. 19, 1745. 27*]

The Passions.—Whenever you would persuade or prevail, address yourself to the passions; it is by them that mankind is to be taken. Cæsar bade his soldiers, at the battle of Pharsalia, aim at the faces of Pompey's men; they did so, and prevailed. I bid you strike at the passions; and if you do, you, too, will prevail. If you can once engage people's pride, love, pity, ambition (or whichever is their prevailing passion) on your side, you need not fear what their reason can do against you. [*Same date.*]

My Dear Boy:—

"Sunt quibus in Satirâ videar nimis acer."

I find, sir, you are one of those; though I cannot imagine why you think so, unless something that I have said, very innocently, has happened to be very applicable to somebody or other of your acquaintance. He makes the satire, who applies it, *qui capit ille facit.* I hope you do not think I meant you, by anything I have said; because, if you do, it seems to imply a consciousness of some guilt, which I dare not presume to suppose, in your case. I know my duty too well, to express, and your merit too well to entertain, such a suspicion. I have not lately read the satirical authors you mention, having very little time here to read. [*Dublin, February, 1746.*]

Inattention. — There is no surer sign in the world of a little, weak mind, than inattention. Whatever is worth doing at all is worth doing well; and nothing can be done well without attention. It is the sure answer of a fool, when you ask him about anything that was said or done where he was present, that "truly he did not mind it." And why did not the fool mind it? What had he else to do there, but to mind what was doing? A man of sense sees, hears, and retains everything that passes where he is. I desire I may never hear you talk of not minding, nor complain, as most fools do, of a treacherous memory. Mind, not only what people say, but how they say it; and, if you have any sagacity, you may discover more truth by your eyes than by your ears. People can say what they will, but they cannot look what they will, and their looks frequently discover what their words are calculated to conceal. The most material knowledge of all — I mean the knowledge of the world — is not to be acquired without great attention. [*Feb. 26, 1746.*]

Women — Classes of Men — Judgment. — Before it is very long, I am of opinion that you will both think and speak more favorably of women than you do now. You seem to think, that, from Eve downward, they have done a great deal of mischief. As for that lady, I give her up to you; but, since her time, history will inform you that men have done much more mischief in the world than women; and, to say the truth, I would not advise you to trust either more than is absolutely necessary. But this I will advise you to, which is, never to attack whole bodies of any kind; for, besides that all general rules have their exceptions, you unnecessarily make yourself a great number of enemies, by attacking a *corps* collectively. Among women, as among men, there are good as well as bad, and it may be full as many, or more, good than among men. This rule holds as to lawyers, soldiers, parsons, courtiers, citizens, etc. They are all men, subject to the same passions and sentiments, differing only in the manner, according to their several educations; and it would be as imprudent as unjust to attack any of them by the lump. Individuals forgive sometimes; but bodies and societies never do. Many young people think it very genteel and witty to abuse the clergy; in which they are extremely mistaken; since, in my opinion, parsons are very like other men, and neither the better nor the worse for wearing a black gown. All general reflections, upon nations and societies, are the trite, threadbare jokes of those who set up for wit without having any, and so have recourse to commonplace. Judge of individuals from your own knowledge of them, and not from their sex, profession, or denomination. [*April, 1746.*]

How to Travel. — I am very well pleased to find that you inform yourself of the particulars of the several places you go through. You do mighty right to see the curiosities in those several places; such as the golden *Bull* at Frankfort, the tun at Heidelberg, etc. Other travellers see them and talk of them; it is very proper to see them, too; but remember, that seeing is the least material object of, travelling; hearing and knowing are the essential points.28 [*September, 1746. From Bath.*]

False Delicacy. — As for the *mauvaise honte,* I hope you are above it; your figure is like other people's, I hope you will take care that your dress is so, too. Why, then, should you be ashamed? Why not go into mixed company with as little concern as you would into your own room? [*Bath, September.*]

The Well Bred Man. — Feels himself firm and easy in all companies; is modest without being bashful, and steady without being impudent; if he is a stranger, he observes, with care, the manners and ways of the people the most esteemed at that place, and conforms to them with complaisance. Instead of finding fault with the customs of that place, and telling the people that the English ones are a thousand times better (as my countrymen are very apt to do), he commends their table, their dress, their houses, and their manners, a little more, it may be, than he really thinks they deserve. But this degree of complaisance is neither criminal nor abject; and is but a small price to pay for the good-will and affection of the people you converse with. As the generality of people are weak enough to be pleased with these little things, those who refuse to please them, so cheaply, are, in my mind, weaker than they. [*Same month, O. S., 1746.*]

"L'Art de Plaire." — There is a very pretty little French book written by L'Abbé de Bellegarde, entitled *"L'Art de Plaire dans la Conversation"*29 ; and, though I confess that it is impossible to reduce the art of pleasing to a system, yet this principle I will lay down, that the desire of pleasing is at least half the art of doing it; the rest depends only upon the manner, which attention, observation, and frequenting good company will teach. But if you are lazy, careless, and indifferent whether you please or not, depend upon it you never will please. [*Same date.*]

Chesterfield's Intention. — Do not think I mean to dictate as a parent; I only mean to advise as a friend, and an indulgent one, too; and do not apprehend that I mean to check your pleasures; of which, on the contrary, I only desire to be the guide, not the censor. Let my experience supply your want of it and clear your way in the progress of your youth of those thorns and briers which scratched and disfigured me in the course of mine. [*Bath, Oct. 4, 1746.*]

His Son's Utter Dependence. — I do not, therefore, so much as hint to you how absolutely dependent you are on me — that you neither have nor can have a shilling in the world but from me; and that as I have no womanish weakness for your person, your merit must, and will, be the only measure of my kindness — I say, I do not hint these things to you because I am convinced that you will act right, upon more noble and generous principles; I mean for the sake of doing right, and out of affection and gratitude to me. [*Same date.*]

No Smattering. — Mr. Pope says, very truly,

"A little knowledge is a dangerous thing;

Drink deep, or taste not the Castalian spring."

And what is called a *smattering* of everything infallibly constitutes a coxcomb. I have often, of late, reflected what an unhappy man I must now have been, if I had not acquired in my youth some fund and taste of learning. What could I have done with myself, at this age, without them? I must, as many ignorant people do, have destroyed my health and faculties by setting away the evenings; or, by wasting them frivolously in the tattle of women's company, must have exposed myself to the ridicule and contempt of those very women; or, lastly, I must have hanged myself, as a man once did, for weariness of putting on and pulling off his shoes and stockings every day. My books, and only my books, are now left me, and I daily find what Cicero says of learning to be true: "Hæc studia" (says he) "adolescentiam alunt, senectutem oblectant, secundas res ornant, adversis perfugium, ac solatium præbent, delectant domi, non impediunt foris, pernoctant nobiscum, peregrinantur, rusticantur." [*October, 1746.*]

Foolish Talk. — The conversation of the ignorant is no conversation, and gives even them no pleasure; they tire of their own sterility, and have not matter enough to furnish them with words to keep up a conversation. [*Same date.*]

World Knowledge. — Do not imagine that the knowledge, which I so much recommend to you, is confined to books, pleasing, useful, and necessary as that knowledge is; but I comprehend in it the great knowledge of the world, still more necessary than that of books. In truth, they assist one another reciprocally; and no man will have either perfectly, who has not both. The knowledge of the world is only to be acquired in the world, and not in a closet. Books alone will never teach it you; but they will suggest many things to your observation, which might otherwise escape you; and your own observations upon mankind, when compared with those which you will find in books, will help you to fix the true point. [*November, 1746.*]

Old Fools.—To know mankind well requires full as much attention and application as to know books, and, it may be, more sagacity and discernment. I am, at this time, acquainted with many elderly people, who have all passed their whole lives in the great world, but with such levity and inattention, that they know no more of it now than they did at fifteen. [*Same date.*]

Introspection.—You must look into people, as well as at them. Almost all people are born with all the passions, to a certain degree; but almost every man has a prevailing one, to which the others are subordinate. Search every one for that ruling passion; pry into the recesses of his heart, and observe the different workings of the same passion in different people. And, when you have found out the prevailing passion of any man, remember never to trust him, where that passion is concerned. Work upon him by it, if you please; but be upon your guard yourself against it, whatever professions he may make you. [*Same date.*]

Young Stanhope's Character.—In the strict scrutiny which I have made into you, I have (thank God) hitherto not discovered any vice of the heart, or any peculiar weakness of the head: but I have discovered laziness, inattention, and indifference; faults which are only pardonable in old men, who, in the decline of life, when health and spirits fail, have a kind of claim to that sort of tranquillity. But a young man should be ambitious to shine, and excel; alert, active, and indefatigable in the means of doing it; and, like Cæsar, "Nil actum reputans, si quid superesset agendum." You seem to want that "vivida vis animi," which spurs and excites most young men to please, to shine, to excel. Without the desire and the pains necessary to be considerable, depend upon it, you never can be so; as, without the desire and attention necessary to please, you never can please. "Nullum numen abest, si sit prudentia," is unquestionably true, with regard to everything except poetry. [*November, 1746.*]

How to Dress.—Take great care always to be dressed like the reasonable people of your own age, in the place where you are; whose dress is never spoken of one way or another, as either too negligent or too much studied. [*Same date.*]

Absent People.—What is commonly called an absent man, is commonly either a very weak or a very affected man; but be he which he will, he is, I am sure, a very disagreeable man in company. He fails in all the common offices of civility; he seems not to know those people to-day, with whom yesterday he appeared to live in intimacy. He takes no part in the general conversation; but, on the contrary, breaks into it from time to time, with some start of his own, as if he waked from a dream. This (as I said before) is a sure indication, either of a mind so weak that it is not able to bear above one object at a time; or so affected, that it would be supposed to be wholly engrossed by, and directed to, some very great and important objects. Sir Isaac Newton, Mr. Locke, and (it may be) five or six more, since the creation of the world, may have had a right to absence, from that intense thought which the things they were investigating required. But if a young man, and a man of the world, who has no such avocations to plead, will claim and exercise that right of absence in company, his pretended right should, in my mind, be turned into an involuntary absence, by his perpetual exclusion out of company. [*Same date.*]

Insult and Injury. — However frivolous a company may be, still, while you are among them, do not show them by your inattention that you think them so; but rather take their tone, and conform in some degree to their weakness, instead of manifesting your contempt for them. There is nothing that people bear more impatiently, or forgive less, than contempt; and an injury is much sooner forgotten than an insult. [*Same date.*]

Flattery. — Most people (I might say all people) have their weaknesses; they have their aversions and their likings to such and such things; so that, if you were to laugh at a man for his aversion to a cat, or cheese (which are common antipathies), or, by inattention and negligence, to let them come in his way where you could prevent it, he would, in the first case, think himself insulted, and, in the second, slighted; and would remember both. Whereas your care to procure for him what he likes, and to remove from him what he hates, shows him that he is at least an object of your attention, flatters his vanity, and makes him possibly more your friend than a more important service would have done. With regard to women, attentions still below these are necessary, and, by the custom of the world, in some measure due, according to the laws of good breeding.

His Letters. — My long and frequent letters, which I send you, in great doubt of their success, put me in mind of certain papers, which you have very lately, and I formerly, sent up to kites, along the string, which we called messengers; some of them the wind used to blow away, others were torn by the string, and but few of them got up and stuck to the kite. But I will content myself now, as I did then, if some of my present messages do but stick to you.

Employment of Time. — I hope you employ your whole time, which few people do; and that you put every moment to profit of some kind or other. I call company, walking, riding, etc., employing one's time, and, upon proper occasions, very usefully; but what I cannot forgive in anybody is sauntering, and doing nothing at all with a thing so precious as time, and so irrecoverable when lost. [*Dec. 9, O. S., 1746. 30*]

Vulgar Pleasures.—Many young people adopt pleasures for which they have not the least taste, only because they are called by that name. They often mistake so totally as to imagine that debauchery is pleasure. You must allow that drunkenness, which is equally destructive to body and mind, is a fine pleasure. Gaming, that draws you into a thousand scrapes, leaves you penniless, and gives you the air and manners of an outrageous madman, is another most exquisite pleasure, is it not? As to running after women, the consequences of that vice are only the loss of one's nose, the total destruction of health, and, not unfrequently, the being run through the body. [*March, 1747.*]

A Gentleman's Pleasures.—The true pleasures of a gentleman are, those of the table, but within the bounds of moderation; good company, that is to say, people of merit; moderate play, which amuses without any interested views; and sprightly, gallant conversations with women of fashion and sense.

These are the real pleasures of a gentleman: which occasion neither sickness, shame, nor repentance. Whatever exceeds them becomes low vice, brutal passion, debauchery, and insanity of mind; all of which, far from giving satisfaction, bring on dishonor and disgrace. Adieu. [*Same date.*]

Virtue and Gold.—Virtue and learning, like gold, have their intrinsic value; but if they are not polished they certainly lose a great deal of their lustre; and even polished brass will pass upon more people than rough gold. What a number of sins does the cheerful, easy, good breeding of the French frequently cover? Many of them want common sense, many more common learning; but, in general, they make up so much by their manner for those defects, that frequently they pass undiscovered. I have often said, and do think, that a Frenchman, who, with a fund of virtue, learning, and good sense, has the manners and good breeding of his country, is the perfection of human nature. [*Same date.*]

Pleasure.—Do not think that I mean to snarl at pleasure like a stoic, or to preach against it like a parson; no, I mean to point it out, and recommend it like an epicurean; I wish you a great deal, and my only view is to hinder you from mistaking it. [*March 6, 1747.*]

Goodness.—You know what virtue is; you may have it if you will; it is in every man's power, and miserable is the man who has it not. [*Same date.*]

The Man of Pleasure.—The character which most young men first aim at is that of a man of pleasure; but they generally take it upon trust; and, instead of consulting their own taste and inclinations, they blindly adopt whatever those with whom they chiefly converse are pleased to call by the name of pleasure; and a *man of pleasure*, in the vulgar acceptation of that phrase, means only a beastly drunkard, an abandoned whoremaster, and a profligate swearer and curser. As it may be of use to you, I am not unwilling, though at the same time ashamed, to own that the vices of my youth proceeded much more from my silly resolution of being what I heard called a man of pleasure, than from my own inclinations. I always naturally hated drinking; and yet I have often drunk, with disgust at the time, attended by great sickness the next day, only because I then considered drinking as a necessary qualification for a fine gentleman and a man of pleasure. [*March 27, 1747.*]

Gambling. — The same as to gaming. I did not want money, and consequently had no occasion to play for it; but I thought play another necessary ingredient in the composition of a man of pleasure, and accordingly I plunged into it, without desire at first; sacrificed a thousand real pleasures to it; and made myself solidly uneasy by it for thirty the best years of my life.

I was even absurd enough, for a little while, to swear, by way of adorning and completing the shining character which I affected; but this folly I soon laid aside upon finding both the guilt and the indecency of it.

Thus seduced by fashion, and blindly adopting nominal pleasures, I lost real ones; and my fortune impaired, and my constitution shattered, are, I must confess, the just punishment of my errors.

Take warning then by them; choose your pleasures for yourself, and do not let them be imposed upon you. Follow nature, and not fashion; weigh the present enjoyment of your pleasures against the necessary consequences of them, and then let your own common-sense determine your choice. [*Same date.*]

A Life of Real Pleasure. — Were I to begin the world again, with the experience which I now have of it, I would lead a life of real, not of imaginary pleasure. I would enjoy the pleasures of the table and of wine; but stop short of the pains inseparably annexed to an excess in either. I would not, at twenty years, be a preaching missionary of abstemiousness and sobriety; and I should let other people do as they would, without formally and sententiously rebuking them for it; but I would be most firmly resolved not to destroy my own faculties and constitution, in complaisance to those who have no regard to their own. I would play to give me pleasure, but not to give me pain; that is, I would play for trifles, in mixed companies, to amuse myself, and conform to custom; but I would take care not to venture for sums which, if I won, I should not be the better for; but which, if I lost, I should deeply regret. [*Same date.*]

Coarse and Vulgar Pleasures.—Does good company care to have a man reeling drunk among them? Or to see another tearing his hair and blaspheming, for having lost at play more than he is able to pay? Or a whoremaster with half a nose, and crippled by coarse and infamous debauchery? No; those who practise, and much more those who brag of them, make no part of good company; and are most unwillingly, if ever, admitted into it.

Fashionable Vices.—A real man of fashion and pleasure observes decency; at least, neither borrows nor affects vices; and, if he unfortunately has any, he gratifies them with choice, delicacy, and secrecy. I have not mentioned the pleasures of the mind (which are the solid and permanent ones), because they do not come under the head of what people commonly call pleasures; which they seem to confine to the senses. The pleasure of virtue, of charity, and of learning is true and lasting pleasure; which I hope you will be well and long acquainted with. Adieu! [*March, 1747.*]

A Fine Edition.—If I am rightly informed, I am now writing to a fine gentleman, in a scarlet coat laced with gold, a brocade waistcoat, and all other suitable ornaments. The natural partiality of every author for his own works, makes me very glad to hear that Mr. Harte has thought this last edition of mine worth so fine a binding; and, as he has bound it in red, and gilt it upon the back, I hope he will take care that it shall be *lettered* too. A showish binding attracts the eyes, and engages the attention of everybody; but with this difference, that women, and men who are like women, mind the binding more than the book, whereas men of sense and learning immediately examine the inside, and, if they find that it does not answer the finery on the outside, they throw it by with the greater indignation and contempt. I hope that when this edition of my works shall be opened and read, the best judges will find connection, consistency, solidity, and spirit in it. Mr. Harte may *recensere* and *emendare* as much as he pleases; but it will be to little purpose if you do not co-operate with him. The work will be imperfect. [*April 3, O. S., 1747.*]

Two Kinds of Salt.—Swiss salt is, I dare say, very good, yet I am apt to suspect it falls a little short of the true Attic salt, in which there was a peculiar quickness and delicacy. The same Attic salt seasoned all Greece; a great deal of it was exported afterwards to Rome, where it was counterfeited by a composition called urbanity, which, in some time, was brought to very near the perfection of the original Attic salt. The more you are powdered with these two kinds of salt the better you will keep, and the more you will be relished. [*April, 1747.*]

One Thing at a Time.—If at a ball, a supper, or a party of pleasure, a man were to be solving, in his own mind, a problem in Euclid, he would be a very bad companion, and make a very poor figure in that company; or if, in studying a problem in his closet, he were to think of a minuet, I am apt to believe that he would make a very poor mathematician. There is time enough for everything in the course of the day, if you do but one thing at once; but there is not time enough in the year, if you will do two things at a time. [*Same date.*]

Letter Writing. — The best models[31] that you can form yourself upon, are Cicero, Cardinal d'Ossat, Madame Sevigné, and Comte Bussy Rabutin. Cicero's epistles to Atticus and to his familiar friends are the best examples that you can imitate, in the friendly and the familiar style. The simplicity and clearness of Cardinal d'Ossat's letters show how letters of business ought to be written; no affected turns, no attempt at wit, obscure or perplex his matter; which is always plainly and clearly stated, as business always should be. For gay and amusing letters, for *enjouement* and *badinage*, there are none that equal Comte Bussy's and Madame Sevigné's. They are so natural, they seem to be the extempore conversations of two people of wit, rather than letters; which are commonly studied, though they ought not to be so. I would advise you to let that book be one in your itinerant library. [*July 20, 1747.*]

Personal Cleanliness. — As you must attend to your manners, so you must not neglect your person; but take care to be very clean, well dressed, and genteel; to have no disagreeable attitudes, nor awkward tricks; which many people use themselves to, and then cannot leave them off. Do you take care to keep your teeth very clean, by washing them constantly every morning, and after every meal? This is very necessary, both to preserve your teeth a great while, and to save you a great deal of pain. Mine have plagued me long, and are now falling out, merely for want of care when I was of your age. Do you dress well, and not too well? Do you consider your air and manner of presenting yourself enough, and not too much? neither negligent nor stiff. All these things deserve a degree of care, a second-rate attention; they give an additional lustre to real merit. My Lord Bacon says that a pleasing figure is a perpetual letter of recommendation. It is certainly an agreeable forerunner of merit and smooths the way for it. [*July 30, 1747.*]

Truth. — Every man seeks for truth; but God only knows who has found it. It is, therefore, as unjust to persecute as it is absurd to ridicule people for those several opinions which they cannot help entertaining upon the conviction of their reason. [*Same date.*]

Lying. — I really know nothing more criminal, more mean, and more ridiculous than lying. It is the production either of malice, cowardice, or vanity; and generally misses of its aim in every one of these views; for lies are always detected, sooner or later. If I tell a malicious lie, in order to affect any man's fortune or character, I may indeed injure him for some time; but I shall be sure to be the greatest sufferer myself at last; for as soon as ever I am detected (and detected I most certainly shall be), I am blasted for the infamous attempt; and whatever is said afterward, to the disadvantage of that person, however true, passes for calumny. If I lie, or equivocate, for it is the same thing, in order to excuse myself for something that I have said or done, and to avoid the danger or the shame that I apprehend from it, I discover at once my fear, as well as my falsehood; and only increase instead of avoiding the danger and the shame; I show myself to be the lowest and the meanest of mankind, and am sure to be always treated as such. Fear, instead of avoiding, invites danger; for concealed cowards will insult known ones. If one has had the misfortune to be in the wrong, there is something noble in frankly owning it; it is the only way of atoning for it, and the only way of being forgiven. Equivocating, evading, shuffling, in order to remove a present danger or inconveniency, is something so mean, and betrays so much fear, that whoever practises them always deserves to be, and often will be, kicked. There is another sort of lies, inoffensive enough in themselves, but wonderfully ridiculous; I mean those lies which a mistaken vanity suggests, that defeat the very end for which they are calculated, and terminate in the humiliation and confusion of their author, who is sure to be detected. These are chiefly narrative and historical lies, all intended to do infinite honor to their author. He is always the hero of his own romances; he has been in dangers from which nobody but himself ever escaped; he has seen with his own eyes whatever other people have heard or read of; he has had more *bonnes fortunes* than ever he knew women; and has ridden more miles post, in one day, than ever courier went in two. He is soon discovered, and as soon becomes the object of universal contempt and ridicule. Remember, then, as long as you live, that nothing but strict truth can carry you through the world, with either your conscience or your honor unwounded. It is not only your duty, but your interest; as a proof of which you may always observe that the greatest fools are the greatest liars. For my own part, I judge of every man's truth by his degree of understanding. [*Sept. 21, 1747.*]

Perception of Character. —Search, therefore, with the greatest care into the characters of all those whom you converse with; endeavor to discover their predominant passions, their prevailing weaknesses, their vanities, their follies, and their humors; with all the right and wrong, wise and silly springs of human actions, which make such inconsistent and whimsical beings of us rational creatures. A moderate share of penetration, with great attention, will infallibly make these necessary discoveries. This is the true knowledge of the world; and the world is a country which nobody ever yet knew by description; one must travel through it one's self to be acquainted with it. The scholar, who in the dust of his closet talks or writes of the world, knows no more of it than that orator did of war, who judiciously endeavored to instruct Hannibal in it. Courts and camps are the only places to learn the world in. [*Oct. 2, 1747.*]

Good Breeding. — Civility, which is a disposition to accommodate and oblige others, is essentially the same in every country; but good breeding, as it is called, which is the manner of exerting that disposition, is different in almost every country, and merely local; and every man of sense imitates and conforms to that local good breeding of the place which he is at. A conformity and flexibility of manners is necessary in the course of the world; that is, with regard to all things which are not wrong in themselves. The *versatile ingenium* is the most useful of all. It can turn itself instantly from one object to another, assuming the proper manner for each. It can be serious with the grave, cheerful with the gay, and trifling with the frivolous. Endeavor, by all means, to accommodate this talent, for it is a very great one. [*Same date.*]

Self-Love. — Do not let your vanity and self-love make you suppose that people become your friends at first sight, or even upon a short acquaintance. Real friendship is a slow grower, and never thrives unless ingrafted upon a stock of known and reciprocal merit. There is another kind of nominal friendship, among young people, which is warm for the time, but, by good luck, of short duration. This friendship is hastily produced, by their being accidentally thrown together, and pursuing the same course of riot and debauchery. A fine friendship, truly! and well cemented by drunkenness and lewdness. It should rather be called a conspiracy against morals and good manners, and be punished as such by the civil magistrate. The next thing to the choice of your friends is the choice of your company. Endeavor, as much as you can, to keep company with people above you. There you rise as much as you sink with people below you; for, as I mentioned before, you are whatever the company you keep is. Do not mistake, when I say company above you, and think that I mean with regard to their birth; that is the least consideration; but I mean with regard to their merit, and the light in which the world considers them. [*Oct. 9, 1747.*]

Good Company. — There are two sorts of good company; one, which is called the *beau monde*, and consists of those people who have the lead in courts, and in the gay part of life; the other consists of those who are distinguished by some peculiar merit, or who excel in some particular and valuable art or science. For my own part, I used to think myself in company as much above me, when I was with Mr. Addison and Mr. Pope, as if I had been with all the princes in Europe. What I mean by low company, which should by all means be avoided, is the company of those, who, absolutely insignificant and contemptible in themselves, think they are honored by being in your company, and who flatter every vice and every folly you have, in order to engage you to converse with them. The pride of being the first of the company is but too common; but it is very silly, and very prejudicial. Nothing in the world lets down a character more than that wrong turn.

You may possibly ask me, whether a man has it always in his power to get into the best company? and how? I say, yes, he has, by deserving it; provided he is but in circumstances which enable him to appear upon the footing of a gentleman. Merit and good breeding will make their way everywhere. Knowledge will introduce him, and good breeding will endear him to the best companies; for, as I have often told you, politeness and good breeding are absolutely necessary to adorn any, or all other good qualities or talents. Without them, no knowledge, no perfection whatsoever, is seen in its best light. The scholar, without good breeding, is a pedant; the philosopher, a cynic; the soldier, a brute; and every man disagreeable. [*Same date.*]

Local Propriety.—Remember that there is a local propriety to be observed in all companies; and that what is extremely proper in one company may be, and often is, highly improper in another. [*Same date.*]

The jokes, the *bon mots*, the little adventures, which may do very well in one company, will seem flat and tedious, when related in another. The particular characters, the habits, the cant of one company may give merit to a word, or a gesture, which would have none at all if divested of those accidental circumstances. Here people very commonly err; and, fond of something that has entertained them in one company, and in certain circumstances, repeat it with emphasis in another, where it is either insipid, or, it may be, offensive, by being ill-timed or misplaced.

Women have, in general, but one object, which is their beauty; upon which, scarce any flattery is too gross for them to follow. Nature has hardly formed a woman ugly enough, to be insensible to flattery upon her person; if her face is so shocking that she must, in some degree, be conscious of it, her figure and her air, she trusts, make ample amends for it. If her figure is deformed, her face, she thinks, counterbalances it. If they are both bad, she comforts herself that she has graces; a certain manner; a *je ne sçais quoi*, still more engaging than beauty. This truth is evident, from the studied and elaborate dress of the ugliest women in the world. An undoubted, uncontested, conscious beauty is, of all women, the least sensible of flattery upon that head; she knows it is her due, and is therefore obliged to nobody for giving it her. She must be flattered upon her understanding; which, though she may possibly not doubt of herself, yet she suspects that men may distrust. [*Oct. 16, 1747.*]

There are a great many people, who think themselves employed all day, and who, if they were to cast up their accounts at night, would find that they had done just nothing. They have read two or three hours, mechanically, without attending to what they read, and, consequently, without either retaining it, or reasoning upon it. From thence they saunter into company, without taking any part in it, and without observing the characters of the persons, or the subjects of the conversation; but are either thinking of some trifle, foreign to the present purpose, or, often, not thinking at all; which silly and idle suspension of thought they would dignify with the name of *absence* and *distraction*. They go afterwards, it may be, to the play, where they gape at the company and the lights; but without minding the very thing they went to, the play. [*Oct. 30, 1747.*]

Action! Action! — Remember the *hoc age*; do what you are about, be that what it will; it is either worth doing well, or not at all. Wherever you are, have (as the low, vulgar expression is) your ears and eyes about you. Listen to everything that is said, and see everything that is done. Observe the looks and countenances of those who speak, which is often a surer way of discovering the truth, than from what they say. [*Same date.*]

Value of Time. — I knew, once, a very covetous, sordid fellow, who used frequently to say: "Take care of the pence, for the pounds will take care of themselves." This was a just and sensible reflection in a miser. I recommend to you to take care of the minutes; for hours will take care of themselves. I am very sure that many people lose two or three hours every day, by not taking care of the minutes. Never think any portion of time, whatsoever, too short to be employed; something or other may always be done in it. [*Nov. 6, 1747.*]

Young People. — The young leading the young is like the blind leading the blind; "they will both fall into the ditch." The only sure guide is he who has often gone the road which you want to go. Let me be that guide; who have gone all roads; and who can consequently point out to you the best. If you ask me why I went any of the bad roads myself? I will answer you, very truly, that it was for want of a good guide; ill example invited me one way, and a good guide was wanting, to show me a better. But if anybody, capable of advising me, had taken the same pains with me, which I have taken, and will continue to take with you, I should have avoided many follies and inconveniences, which undirected youth ran me into. My father was neither desirous nor able to advise me; which is what, I hope, you cannot say of yours. [*Nov. 24, 1747.*]

From Home. — I send you, by a person who sets out this day for Leipsic, a small packet from your mamma, containing some valuable things which you left behind; to which I have added, by way of New Year's gift, a very pretty toothpick case; and, by the way, pray take great care of your teeth, and keep them extremely clean. I have likewise sent you the Greek roots, lately translated into English from the French of the Port Royal. Inform yourself what the Port Royal is. To conclude with a quibble: I hope you will not only feed upon these Greek roots, but likewise digest them perfectly. Adieu. [*Same date.*]

Time. — There is nothing which I more wish that you should know, and which fewer people do know, than the true use and value of time. It is in everybody's mouth; but in few people's practice. Every fool, who slatterns away his whole time in nothings, utters, however, some trite commonplace sentence, of which there are millions, to prove, at once, the value and the fleetness of time. The sundials, likewise, all over Europe, have some ingenious inscription to that effect; so that nobody squanders away their time without hearing and seeing, daily, how necessary it is to employ it well, and how irrecoverable it is if lost. But all these admonitions are useless, where there is not a fund of good sense and reason to suggest them, rather than receive them. By the manner in which you now tell me that you employ your time, I flatter myself that you have that fund: that is the fund which will make you rich indeed. I do not, therefore, mean to give you a critical essay upon the use and abuse of time; I will only give you some hints, with regards to the use of one particular period of that long time which, I hope, you have before you; I mean, the next two years. Remember then, that whatever knowledge you do not solidly lay the foundation of before you are eighteen, you will never be master of while you breathe. [*Dec. 11, 1747.*]

Knowledge. — Knowledge is a comfortable and necessary retreat and shelter for us in an advanced age; and if we do not plant it while young, it will give us no shade when we grow old. [*Same date.*]

A Classical Student. — I knew a gentleman who was so good a manager of his time that he would not even lose that small portion of it which the calls of nature obliged him to pass in the necessary house; but gradually went through all the Latin poets in those moments. He bought, for example, a common edition of Horace, of which he tore off gradually a couple of pages, read them first, and then sent them down a sacrifice to Cloacina; this was so much time fairly gained. [*Same date.*]

Young Stanhope. — Hitherto I have discovered nothing wrong in your heart, or your head; on the contrary, I think I see sense in the one, and sentiments in the other. This persuasion is the only motive of my present affection; which will either increase or diminish, according to your merit or demerit. If you have the knowledge, the honor, and the probity which you may have, the marks and warmth of my affection shall amply reward them. [*Dec. 18, 1747.*]

Fashionable Ladies. — The company of women of fashion will improve your manners, though not your understanding; and that complaisance and politeness, which are so useful in men's company, can only be acquired in women's. [*Dec. 29, 1747.*]

Talent and Breeding. — Remember always, what I have told you a thousand times, that all the talents in the world will want all their lustre, and some part of their use too, if they are not adorned with that easy good breeding, that engaging manner, and those graces which seduce and prepossess people in your favor at first sight. A proper care of your person is by no means to be neglected; always extremely clean; upon proper occasions, fine. Your carriage genteel, and your motions graceful. Take particular care of your manner and address, when you present yourself in company. Let them be respectful without meanness, easy without too much familiarity, genteel without affectation, and insinuating without any seeming art or design. [*Same date.*]

Polish. — Now, though I would not recommend to you to go into woman's company in search of solid knowledge or judgment, yet it has its use in other respects; for it certainly polishes the manners, and gives *une certaine tournure*, which is very necessary in the course of the world; and which Englishmen have generally less of than any people in the world. [*Jan. 2, 1748.*]

A Good Supper. — I cannot say that your suppers are luxurious, but you must own they are solid; and a quart of soup, and two pounds of potatoes, will enable you to pass the night without great impatience for your breakfast next morning. One part of your supper (the potatoes) is the constant diet of my old friends and countrymen, the Irish, who are the healthiest and the strongest men that I know in Europe. [*Same date.*]

A Greek Professor. — Since you do not care to be an assessor of the Imperial Chamber, and desire an establishment in England; what do you think of being Greek professor at one of our universities? It is a very pretty sinecure, and requires very little knowledge (much less than, I hope, you have already) of that language. [*Jan. 15, 1748.*]

A Politician. — Mr. Harte tells me that you set up for a πολιτικὸς ἀνὴρ; if so, I presume it is in the view of succeeding me in my office; which I will very willingly resign to you, whenever you shall call upon me for it. But, if you intend to be the πολιτικὸς ἀνὴρ, or the βεληφόρος ἀνὴρ, there are some trifling circumstances, upon which you should previously take your resolution. The first of which is, to be fit for it; and then, in order to be so, make yourself master of ancient and modern history and languages. To know perfectly the constitution, and form of government of every nation; the growth and decline of ancient and modern empires; and to trace out and reflect upon the causes of both. To know the strength, the riches, and the commerce of every country. These little things, trifling as they may seem, are yet very necessary for a politician to know; and which therefore, I presume, you will condescend to apply yourself to. There are some additional qualifications necessary, in the practical part of business, which may deserve some consideration in your leisure moments; such as an absolute command of your temper, so as not to be provoked to passion, upon any account: patience, to hear frivolous, impertinent, and unreasonable applications: with address enough to refuse, without offending; or, by your manner of granting, to double the obligation: dexterity enough to conceal a truth, without telling a lie: sagacity enough to read other people's countenances: and serenity enough not to let them discover anything by yours; a seeming frankness, with a real reserve. These are the rudiments of a politician; the world must be your grammar.

Three mails are now due from Holland, so that I have no letters from you to acknowledge. I therefore conclude with recommending myself to your favor and protection when you succeed. [*Same date.*]

Congealed Speech.—I find by Mr. Harte's last letter, that many of my letters to you and him have been frozen up in their way to Leipsic; the thaw has, I suppose, by this time set them at liberty to pursue their journey to you, and you will receive a glut of them at once. Hudibras alludes, in this verse,

"Like words congeal'd in northern air,"

to a vulgar notion, that in Greenland words were frozen in their utterance, and that upon a thaw a very mixed conversation was heard in the air of all those words set at liberty. [*Jan. 29, 1748.*]

Political Ignorance of the English.—We are in general in England ignorant of foreign affairs and of the interests, views, pretensions, and policy of other courts. That part of knowledge never enters into our thoughts, nor makes part of our education; for which reason we have fewer proper subjects for foreign commissions than any other country in Europe; and, when foreign affairs happen to be debated in Parliament, it is incredible with how much ignorance. The harvest of foreign affairs being then so great, and the laborers so few, if you make yourself master of them, you will make yourself necessary: first as a foreign, and then as a domestic minister for that department. [*Feb. 9, 1748.*]

My Lord's Dislike of Valets.—I would neither have your new man nor him whom you have already, put out of livery, which makes them both impertinent and useless. I am sure that as soon as you shall have taken the other servant, your present man will press extremely to be out of livery, and valet de chambre, which is as much as to say, that he will curl your hair and shave you, but not condescend to do anything else. Therefore I advise you never to have a servant out of livery; and though you may not always think proper to carry the servant who dresses you abroad in the rain and dirt behind a coach or before a chair, you keep it in your power to do so, if you please, by keeping him in livery. [*Feb. 13, 1748.*]

Learned Leisure.—The first use that I made of my liberty was to come hither [Bath], where I arrived yesterday. My health, though not fundamentally bad, yet, for want of proper attention of late, wanted some repairs, which these waters never fail giving it. I shall drink them a month, and return to London, there to enjoy the comforts of social life, instead of groaning under the load of business. I have given the description of the life that I propose to lead for the future in this motto, which I have put up in the frize (*sic*) of my library in my new house:

"Nunc veterum libris, nunc somno, et inertibus horis

Ducere sollicitæ jucunda oblivia vitæ."

I must observe to you upon this occasion, that the uninterrupted satisfaction which I expect to find in that library will be chiefly owing to my having employed some part of my life well at your age. I wish I had employed it better, and my satisfaction would now be complete. [*Feb. 16, 1748.*]

Waste of Time.—I, who have been behind the scenes, both of pleasure and business, and have seen all the springs and pulleys of those decorations which astonish and dazzle the audience, retire, not only without regret, but with contentment and satisfaction. But what I do, and ever shall, regret, is the time which, while young, I lost in mere idleness, and in doing nothing. This is the common effect of the inconsideracy of youth, against which I beg you will be most carefully upon your guard. The value of moments, when cast up, is immense, if well employed; if thrown away, their loss is irrecoverable. Every moment may be put to some use, and that with much more pleasure than if unemployed. Do not imagine that by the employment of time I mean an uninterrupted application to serious studies. No; pleasures are, at proper times, both as necessary and as useful; they fashion and form you for the world; they teach you characters, and show you the human heart in its unguarded minutes. But then remember to make that use of them. I have known many people, from laziness of mind, go through both pleasure and business with equal inattention; neither enjoying the one, nor doing the other; thinking themselves men of pleasure because they were mingled with those who were, and men of business, because they had business to do, though they did not do it. Whatever you do, do it to the purpose; do it thoroughly, not superficially. *Approfondissez*; go to the bottom of things. Anything half done, or half known, is, in my mind, neither done nor known at all. Nay worse, for it often misleads. There is hardly any place, or any company, where you may not gain knowledge, if you please; almost everybody knows some one thing, and is glad to talk upon that one thing. [*Same date.*]

Proper Inquisitiveness. — Seek, and you will find, in this world as well as in the next. See everything, inquire into everything; and you may excuse your curiosity and the questions you ask, which otherwise might be thought impertinent by your manner of asking them; for most things depend a great deal upon the manner. As, for example, *I am afraid that I am very troublesome with my questions; but nobody can inform me so well as you*; or something of that kind. [*Same date.*]

Religion to be Respected. — But when you frequent places of public worship, as I would have you go to all the different ones you meet with, remember that, however erroneous, they are none of them objects of laughter and ridicule. Honest error is to be pitied, not ridiculed. The object of all the public worships in the world is the same; it is that great eternal Being who created everything. The different manners of worship are by no means subjects of ridicule. Each sect thinks its own the best; and I know no infallible judge, in this world, to decide which is the best. [*Same date.*]

Use a Note-Book. — Make the same inquiries, wherever you are, concerning the revenues, the military establishment, the trade, the commerce, and the police of every country. And you would do well to keep a blank paper book, which the Germans call an *album*; and there, instead of desiring, as they do, every fool they meet with to scribble something, write down all these things, as soon as they come to your knowledge from good authorities. [*Same date.*]

Lord Chesterfield's Care. — I have now but one anxiety left, which is concerning you. I would have you be, what I know nobody is, perfect. As that is impossible, I would have you as near perfection as possible. I know nobody in a fairer way toward it than yourself, if you please. Never were so much pains taken for anybody's education as for yours; and never had anybody those opportunities of knowledge and improvement which you have had, and still have. I hope, I wish, I doubt, and I fear alternately. This only I am sure of, that you will prove either the greatest pain, or the greatest pleasure of, yours always truly. [*Same date.*]

Pedants.—Others, to show their learning, or often from the prejudices of a school education, where they hear of nothing else, are always talking of the ancients, as something more than men, and of the moderns as something less. They are never without a classic or two in their pockets; they stick to the old good sense; they read none of the modern trash; and will show you plainly that no improvement has been made, in any one art or science, these last seventeen hundred years. I would by no means have you disown your acquaintance with the ancients; but still less would I have you brag of an exclusive intimacy with them. Speak of the moderns without contempt, and of the ancients without idolatry; judge them all by their merits, but not by their ages; and if you happen to have an Elzevir classic in your pocket, neither show it nor mention it. [*Bath, Feb. 22, 1748.*]

Blindness to Heroism.—Take into your consideration, if you please, cases seemingly analogous; but take them as helps only, not as guides. We are really so prejudiced by our educations that, as the ancients deified their heroes, we deify their madmen; of which, with all due regard to antiquity, I take Leonidas and Curtius to have been two distinguished ones. And yet a solid pedant would, in a speech in Parliament, relative to a tax of twopence in the pound, upon some commodity or other, quote those two heroes as examples of what we ought to do and suffer for our country. [*Same date.*]

Injudicious Learning.—I have known these absurdities carried so far by people of injudicious learning, that I should not be surprised if some of them were to propose, while we were at war with the Gauls, that a number of geese should be kept in the Tower, upon account of the infinite advantage which Rome received, in a parallel case, from a certain number of geese in the Capitol. This way of reasoning and this way of speaking will always form a poor politician and a puerile declaimer. [*Same date.*]

How "to Wear" Learning.—Wear your learning like your watch, in a private pocket; and do not pull it out and strike it, merely to show that you have one. If you are asked what o'clock it is, tell it, but do not proclaim it hourly and unasked, like the watchman. [*Same date.*]

The Graces.—A thousand little things, not separately to be defined, conspire to form these graces, this *je ne sais quoi* that always pleases. A pretty person, genteel motions, a proper degree of dress, an harmonious voice, something open and cheerful in the countenance, but without laughing; a distinct and properly varied manner of speaking; all these things, and many others, are necessary ingredients in the composition of the pleasing *je ne sais quoi*, which everybody feels, though nobody can describe. Observe carefully, then, what displeases or pleases you, in others, and be persuaded, that, in general, the same things will please or displease others, in you. Having mentioned laughing, I must particularly warn you against it; and

I could heartily wish that you may often be seen to smile, but never heard to laugh while you live. Frequent and loud laughter is the characteristic of folly and ill-manners; it is the manner in which the mob express their silly joy at silly things; and they call it being merry. In my mind, there is nothing so illiberal and so ill-bred as audible laughter. [*March 9, 1748.*]

The Folly of Laughter. — True wit or sense never yet made anybody laugh; they are above it; they please the mind and give a cheerfulness to the countenance. But it is low buffoonery or silly accidents that always excite laughter; and that is what people of sense and breeding should show themselves above. A man's going to sit down, in the supposition that he has a chair behind him, and falling down upon his breech for want of one, sets a whole company a-laughing, when all the wit in the world would not do it; a plain proof, in my mind, how low and unbecoming a thing laughter is. Not to mention the disagreeable noise that it makes, and the shocking distortion of the face that it occasions. Laughter is easily restrained by a very little reflection; but as it is generally connected with the idea of gaiety, people do not enough attend to its absurdity. I am neither of a melancholy nor a cynical disposition; and am as willing and as apt to be pleased as anybody; but I am sure that, since I have had the full use of my reason, nobody has ever heard me laugh. [*Same date.*]

The Mind. — It requires, also, a great deal of exercise, to bring it to a state of health and vigor. Observe the difference there is between minds cultivated and minds uncultivated, and you will, I am sure, think that you cannot take too much pains, nor employ too much of your time in the culture of your own. A drayman is probably born with as good organs as Milton, Locke, or Newton; but, by culture, they are much more above him than he is above his horse. Sometimes, indeed, extraordinary geniuses have broken out by the force of nature, without the assistance of education; but those instances are too rare for anybody to trust to; and even they would make a much greater figure if they had the advantage of education into the bargain. [*April 1, 1748.*]

See all Things. — At least, see everything that you can see, and know everything that you can know of it, by asking questions. See likewise everything at the fair, from operas and plays down to the Savoyards' rareeshows. Everything is worth seeing once; and the more one sees, the less one either wonders or admires. [*April 15, 1748.*]

Falsehood Universal. — Falsehood and dissimulation are certainly to be found at courts; but where are they not to be found? Cottages have them as well as courts; only with worse manners. A couple of neighboring farmers, in a village, will contrive and practice as many tricks to overreach each other at the next market, or to supplant each other in the favor of the squire, as any two courtiers can do to supplant each other in the favor of their prince. Whatever poets may write, or fools believe, of rural innocence and truth, and of the perfidy of courts, this is most undoubtedly true—that shepherds and ministers are both men; their nature and passions the same, the modes of them only different. [*May 10, 1748.*]

Vulgar Scoffers.—Religion is one of their favorite topics; it is all priestcraft; and an invention contrived and carried on by priests, of all religions, for their own power and profit; from this absurd and false principle flow the commonplace, insipid jokes and insults upon the clergy. With these people, every priest, of every religion, is either a public or a concealed unbeliever, drunkard, and whoremaster; whereas I conceive that priests are extremely like other men, and neither the better nor the worse for wearing a gown or a surplice; but, if they are different from other people, probably it is rather on the side of religion and morality, or at least decency, from their education and manner of life. [*Same date.*]

Wit—False and Vulgar.—Another common topic for false wit and cold raillery is matrimony. Every man and his wife hate each other cordially, whatever they may pretend, in public, to the contrary. The husband certainly wishes his wife at the devil, and the wife certainly cuckolds her husband. Whereas I presume that men and their wives neither love nor hate each other the more upon account of the form of matrimony which has been said over them. The cohabitation, indeed, which is the consequence of matrimony, makes them either love or hate more, accordingly as they respectively deserve it; but that would be exactly the same, between any man and woman, who lived together without being married. [*Same date.*]

Snubbing a "Wit."—I always put these pert jackanapeses out of countenance, by looking extremely grave, when they expect that I should laugh at their pleasantries; and by saying *Well, and so*; as if they had not done, and that the sting were still to come. This disconcerts them, as they have no resources in themselves, and have but one set of jokes to live upon. [*Same date.*]

Method and Manner.—The manner of doing things is often more important than the things themselves; and the very same thing may become either pleasing or offensive, by the manner of saying or doing it. *Materiam superabat opus* is often said of works of sculpture, where though the materials were valuable, as silver, gold, etc., the workmanship was still more so. [*Same date.*]

Chesterfield's Proposed Aim.—The end which I propose by your education, and which (if you please) I shall certainly attain, is to unite in you the knowledge of a scholar with the manners of a courtier; and to join, what is seldom joined in any of my countrymen, books and the world. They are commonly twenty years old before they have spoken to anybody above their schoolmaster and the fellows of their college. If they happen to have learning, it is only Greek and Latin; but not one word of modern history or modern languages. Thus prepared, they go abroad, as they call it; but, in truth, they stay at home all that while; for being very awkward, confoundedly ashamed, and not speaking the languages, they go into no foreign company, at least none good; but dine and sup with one another only, at the tavern. Such examples, I am sure, you will not imitate, but even carefully avoid. [*Same date.*]

Good Company. — You will always take care to keep the best company in the place where you are, which is the only use of travelling; and (by the way) the pleasures of a gentleman are only to be found in the best company; for that riot which low company, most falsely and impudently, call pleasure, is only the sensuality of a swine. [*Same date.*]

Manly Deference to Rank. — People of a low, obscure education cannot stand the rays of greatness; they are frightened out of their wits when kings and great men speak to them; they are awkward, ashamed, and do not know what nor how to answer, whereas: *les honnêtes gens* are not dazzled by superior rank; they know and pay all the respect that is due to it; but they do it without being disconcerted; and can converse just as easily with a king as with any one of his subjects. That is the great advantage of being introduced young into good company, and being used early to converse with one's superiors. How many men have I seen here, who, after having had the full benefit of an English education, first at school and then at the university, when they have been presented to the king, did not know whether they stood upon their heads or their heels. [*May 17, 1748.*]

Vulgarity and Good Breeding at Court. — If the king spoke to them, they were annihilated; they trembled, endeavored to put their hands in their pockets and missed them, let their hats fall, and were ashamed to take them up; and, in short, put themselves in every attitude but the right, that is, the easy and natural one. The characteristic of a well-bred man is, to converse with his inferiors without insolence, and with his superiors with respect and with ease. He talks to kings without concern; he trifles with women of the first condition, with familiarity, gaiety, but respect; and converses with his equals, whether he is acquainted with them or not, upon general, common topics, that are not, however, quite frivolous, without the least concern of mind or awkwardness of body; neither of which can appear to advantage, but when they are perfectly easy. [*Same date.*]

Filial Love to the Mother.—You owe her not only duty, but likewise great obligations, for her care and tenderness; and consequently cannot take too many opportunities of showing your gratitude.32 [*Same date.*]

Consider your own Situation.—You have not the advantage of rank and fortune to bear you up; I shall, very probably, be out of the world before you can properly be said to be in it. What then will you have to rely on but your own merit? That alone must raise you, and that alone will raise you, if you have but enough of it. I have often heard and read of oppressed and unrewarded merit, but I have oftener (I might say always) seen great merit make its way, and meet with its reward, to a certain degree at least, in spite of all difficulties. By merit I mean the moral virtues, knowledge, and manners; as to the moral virtues, I say nothing to you; they speak best for themselves; nor can I suspect that they want any recommendation with you; I will, therefore, only assure you that, without them you will be most unhappy. [*May 27, 1748.*]

Diplomatic Education.—You must absolutely speak all the modern languages, as purely and correctly as the natives of the respective countries; for whoever does not speak a language perfectly and easily, will never appear to advantage in conversation, nor treat with others in it upon equal terms. As for French, you have it very well already; and must necessarily, from the universal usage of that language, know it better and better every day; so that I am in no pain about that. German, I suppose, you know pretty well by this time, and will be quite master of it before you leave Leipsic; at least I am sure you may. Italian and Spanish will come in their turns; and, indeed, they are both so easy, to one who knows Latin and French, that neither of them will cost you much time or trouble. [*Same date.*]

Advantages of Manners.—Manners, though the last, and it may be the least ingredient of real merit, are, however, very far from being useless in its composition; they adorn, and give an additional force and lustre to both virtue and knowledge. They prepare and smooth the way for the progress of both; and are, I fear, with the bulk of mankind, more engaging than either. Remember, then, the infinite advantage of manners; cultivate and improve your own to the utmost; good sense will suggest the great rules to you, good company will do the rest. [*Same date.*]

Foreign Ministers.—You are the only one I ever knew, of this country, whose education was, from the beginning, calculated for the department of foreign affairs; in consequence of which, if you will invariably pursue, and diligently qualify yourself for that object, you may make yourself absolutely necessary to the government; and, after having received orders as a minister abroad, send orders, in your turn, as Secretary of State at home. Most of our ministers abroad have taken up that department occasionally, without having ever thought of foreign affairs before—many of them, without speaking any one foreign language; and all of them without the manners which are absolutely necessary towards being well received and making a figure at foreign courts. [*Same date.*]

How to be Considerable.—Upon the whole, if you have a mind to be considerable, and to shine hereafter, you must labor hard now. No quickness of parts, no vivacity, will do long, or go far, without a solid fund of knowledge; and that fund of knowledge will amply repay all the pains that you can take in acquiring it. Reflect seriously, within yourself, upon all this, and ask yourself, whether I can have any view, but your interest, in all that I recommend to you. [*Same date.*]

The Pope's Power.—Indulgences stood instead of armies, in the times of ignorance and bigotry; but now that mankind is better informed, the spiritual authority of the Pope is not only less regarded, but even despised, by the Catholic princes themselves; and his holiness is actually little more than Bishop of Rome. [*May 31, 1748.*]

Papal Virtues.—Alexander VI., together with his natural son, Cæsar Borgia, was famous for his wickedness, in which he, and his son too, surpassed all imagination. Their lives are well worth your reading. They were poisoned themselves by the poisoned wine which they had prepared for others; the father died of it, but Cæsar recovered.

Sixtus V. was the son of a swineherd, and raised himself to the popedom by his abilities; he was a great knave, but an able and a singular one.

Here is history enough for to-day. [*Same date.*]

Awkward Speech.—Good God! if this ungraceful and disagreeable manner of speaking had, either by your negligence or mine, become habitual to you, as in a couple of years more it would have been, what a figure would you have made in company, or in a public assembly? Who would have liked you in the one, or have attended to you in the other? Read what Cicero and Quintilian say of enunciation, and see what a stress they lay upon the gracefulness of it; nay, Cicero goes further, and even maintains that a good figure is necessary for an orator; and, particularly, that he must not be *vastus*; that is, overgrown and clumsy. He shows by it that he knew mankind well, and knew the powers of an agreeable figure and a graceful manner. [*June 21, 1748.*]

Enunciation—Eloquence.—Your figure is a good one; you have no natural defect in the organs of speech; your address may be engaging, and your manner of speaking graceful, if you will; so that, if they are not so, neither I nor the world can ascribe it to any thing but your want of parts. What is the constant and just observation as to all actors upon the stage? Is it not, that those who have the best sense always speak the best, though they may happen not to have the best voices? They will speak plainly, distinctly, and with the proper emphasis, be their voices ever so bad. Had Roscius spoken *quick, thick,* and *ungracefully,* I will answer for it that Cicero would not have thought him worth the oration which he made in his favor. Words were given us to communicate our ideas by; and there must be something inconceivably absurd in uttering them in such a manner as that either people cannot understand them, or will not desire to understand them. I tell you truly and sincerely that I shall judge of your parts by your speaking gracefully or ungracefully. If you have parts, you will never be at rest till you have brought yourself to a habit of speaking most gracefully; for I aver that it is in your power. [*Same date.*]

Articulation. — You will take care to open your teeth when you speak; to articulate every word distinctly; and to beg of Mr. Harte, Mr. Eliot, or whomever you speak to, to remind and stop you, if ever you fall into the rapid and unintelligible mutter. You will even read aloud to yourself, and tune your utterance to your own ear; and read at first much slower than you need to do, in order to correct yourself of that shameful trick of speaking faster than you ought.

Proper Carriage. — Next to graceful speaking, a genteel carriage and a graceful manner of presenting yourself are extremely necessary, for they are extremely engaging; and carelessness in these points is much more unpardonable in a young fellow than affectation. It shows an offensive indifference about pleasing. I am told by one here, who has seen you lately, that you are awkward in your motions, and negligent of your person. I am sorry for both; and so will you, when it will be too late, if you continue so some time longer. Awkwardness of carriage is very alienating, and a total negligence of dress and air is an impertinent insult upon custom and fashion. [*Same date.*]

Desert and Reward. — Deserve a great deal, and you shall have a great deal; deserve little, and you shall have but a little; and be good for nothing at all, and I assure you, you shall have nothing at all.

Solid knowledge, as I have often told you, is the first and great foundation of your future fortune and character; for I never mention to you the two much greater points of religion and morality, because I cannot possibly suspect you as to either of them. [*July 1, 1748.*]

No One Contemptible. — Be convinced that there are no persons so insignificant and inconsiderable, but may some time or other, and in something or other, have it in their power to be of use to you; which they certainly will not, if you have once shown them contempt. [*Same date.*]

The Folly of Contempt. — Wrongs are often given, but contempt never is. Our pride remembers it forever. It implies a discovery of weaknesses, which we are much more careful to conceal than crimes. Many a man will confess his crimes to a common friend, but I never knew a man who would tell his silly weaknesses to his most intimate one. As many a friend will tell us our faults without reserve, who will not so much as hint at our follies; that discovery is too mortifying to our self-love, either to tell another, or to be told of, one's self. You must, therefore, never expect to hear of your weaknesses, or your follies, from anybody but me; those I will take pains to discover, and whenever I do, I shall tell you of them. [*Same date.*]

Good Nature. — Your school-fellow, Lord Pulteney, set out last week for Holland, and will, I believe, be at Leipsic soon after this letter. You will take care to be extremely civil to him, and to do him any service that you can, while you stay there; let him know that I wrote you to do so. As being older, he should know more than you; in that case, take pains to get up to him; but if he does not, take care not to let him feel his inferiority. He will find it out of himself, without your endeavors; and that cannot be helped; but nothing is more insulting, more mortifying, and less forgiven, than avowedly to take pains to make a man feel a mortifying inferiority in knowledge, rank, fortune, etc. In the two last articles it is unjust, they not being in his power; and in the first it is both ill-bred and ill-natured. Good breeding and good nature do incline us rather to help and raise people up to ourselves, than to mortify and depress them, and, in truth, our own private interest concurs in it, as it is making ourselves so many friends, instead of so many enemies. [*July 6, 1748.*]

Les Attentions. — The constant practice of what the French call *les attentions* is a most necessary ingredient in the art of pleasing; they flatter the self-love of those to whom they are shown; they engage, they captivate, more than things of much greater importance. The duties of social life every man is obliged to discharge; but these attentions are voluntary acts, the free-will offerings of good breeding and good nature; they are received, remembered, and returned as such. Women, particularly, have a right to them; and any omission in that respect is downright ill breeding. [*Same date.*]

An Educational Test. — Tell me what Greek and Latin books you can now read with ease. Can you open Demosthenes at a venture, and understand him? Can you get through an oration of Cicero, or a satire of Horace, without difficulty? What German book do you read to make yourself master of that language? And what French books do you read for your amusement? Pray give me a particular and true account of all this; for I am not indifferent as to any one thing that relates to you. [*Same date.*]

Lazy Minds.—There are two sorts of understandings; one of which hinders a man from ever being considerable, and the other commonly makes him ridiculous; I mean the lazy mind, and the trifling, frivolous mind. Yours, I hope, is neither. The lazy mind will not take the trouble of going to the bottom of anything; but, discouraged by the difficulties (and everything worth knowing or having is attended with some), stops short, contents itself with easy and, consequently, superficial knowledge, and prefers a great degree of ignorance to a small degree of trouble. These people either think or represent most things as impossible; whereas few things are so to industry and activity. [*July 26, 1748.*]

Resolution. — But difficulties seem to them (lazy people) impossibilities, or at least they pretend to think them so, by way of excuse for their laziness. An hour's attention to the same object is too laborious for them; they take everything in the light in which it first presents itself, never considering it in all its different views; and, in short, never think it thorough. The consequence of this is, that when they come to speak upon these subjects before people who have considered them with attention, they only discover their own ignorance and laziness, and lay themselves open to answers that put them in confusion. Do not then be discouraged by the first difficulties, but *contra audentior ito*; and resolve to go to the bottom of all those things which every gentleman ought to know well. [*Same date.*]

Conversation.—When you are in company, bring the conversation to some useful subject, but *à portée* of that company. Points of history, matters of literature, the customs of particular countries, the several orders of knighthood, as Teutonic, Maltese, etc., are surely better subjects of conversation than the weather, dress, or fiddle-faddle stories, that carry no information along with them. The characters of kings and great men are only to be learned in conversation; for they are never fairly written during their lives. [*Same date.*]

Always Ask.—Never be ashamed nor afraid of asking questions; for if they lead to information, and if you accompany them with some excuse, you will never be reckoned an impertinent or rude questioner. All those things, in the common course of life, depend entirely upon the manner; and in that respect the vulgar saying is true, "That one man may better steal a horse, than another look over the hedge." [*Same date.*]

Two Heads.—I am very glad that Mr. Lyttelton approves of my new house, and particularly of my *Canonical* 33 pillars. My bust of Cicero is a very fine one, and well preserved; it will have the best place in my library, unless, at your return, you bring me over as good a modern head of your own, which I should like still better. I can tell you that I shall examine it as attentively as ever antiquary did an old one. [*Same date.*]

A Picture. — Duval, the jeweler, is arrived, and was with me three or four days ago. You will easily imagine that I asked him a few questions concerning you; and I will give you the satisfaction of knowing that, upon the whole, I was very well pleased with the account he gave me. But, though he seemed to be much in your interest, yet he fairly owned to me that your utterance was rapid, thick, and ungraceful. I can add nothing to what I have already said upon this subject; but I can and do repeat the absolute necessity of speaking distinctly and gracefully.34 [*Aug. 2, 1748.*]

Diet. — He tells me that you are pretty fat for one of your age; this you should attend to in a proper way; for if, while very young, you should grow fat, it would be troublesome, unwholesome, and ungraceful; you should therefore, when you have time, take very strong exercise, and in your diet avoid fattening things. All malt liquors fatten, or at least bloat; and I hope you do not deal much in them. [*Same date.*]

Be Natural. — I have this moment received your letter of the 4th, N. S., and have only time to tell you, that I can by no means agree to your cutting off your hair. I am very sure that your headaches cannot proceed from thence. And as for the pimples upon your head, they are only owing to the heat of the season; and consequently will not last long. But your own hair is, at your age, such an ornament, and a wig, however well made, such a disguise, that I will upon no account whatsoever have you cut off your hair. Nature did not give it you for nothing, still less to cause you the headache. Mr. Eliot's hair grew so ill and bushy, that he was in the right to cut it off; but you have not the same reason. [*Same date.*]

Buying Books. — Mr. Harte wrote me word some time ago, and Mr. Eliot confirms it now, that you employ your pin-money in a very different manner from that in which pin-money35 is commonly lavished. Not in gewgaws and baubles, but in buying good and useful books. This is an excellent symptom, and gives me very good hopes. Go on thus, my dear boy, but for these two next years, and I ask no more. You must then make such a figure, and such a fortune in the world, as I wish you, and as I have taken all these pains to enable you to do. After that time, I allow you to be as idle as ever you please; because I am sure that you will not then please to be so at all. The ignorant and the weak only are idle; but those, who have once acquired a good stock of knowledge, always desire to increase it. Knowledge is like power, in this respect, that those who have the most, are most desirous of having more. It does not clog, by possession, but increases desires; which is the case of very few pleasures. [*Aug. 23, 1748.*]

Gratitude to a Tutor. — Upon receiving this congratulatory letter, and reading your own praises, I am sure that it must naturally occur to you, how great a share of them you owe to Mr. Harte's care and attention; and, consequently, that your regard and affection for him must increase, if there be room for it, in proportion as you reap, which you do daily, the fruits of his labors. [*Same date.*]

Historical Faith. — Take nothing for granted, upon the bare authority of the author; but weigh and consider, in your own mind, the probability of the facts, and the justness of the reflections. Consult different authors upon the same facts, and form your opinion upon the greater or lesser degree of probability arising from the whole, which, in my mind, is the utmost stretch of historical faith, certainty (I fear) not being to be found. [*Aug. 30, 1748.*]

Good and Bad Mixed. — The best have something bad, and something little; the worst have something good, and sometimes something great; for I do not believe what Valleius Paterculus (for the sake of saying a pretty thing) says of Scipio, "Qui nihil non laudandum aut fecit, aut dixit, aut sensit." [*Same date.*]

The Ruling Passion. — Seek for their particular merit, their predominant passion, or their prevailing weakness, and you will then know what to bait your hook with, to catch them. Man is a composition of so many and such various ingredients, that it requires both time and care to analyze him: for though we have, all, the same ingredients in our general composition, as reason, will, passions, and appetites, yet the different proportions and combinations of them, in each individual, produce that infinite variety of characters, which, in some particular or other, distinguishes every individual from another. Reason ought to direct the whole, but seldom does. [*Sept. 5, 1748.*]

Bruyère and Rochefoucault. — I will recommend to your attentive perusal, now you are going into the world, two books, which will let you as much into the characters of men as books can do. I mean "Les Réflexions Morales de Monsieur de la Rochefoucault," and "Les Caractères de la Bruyère": but remember, at the same time, that I only recommend them to you as the best general maps, to assist you in your journey, and not as marking out every particular turning and winding that you will meet with. There, your own sagacity and observation must come to their aid. La Rochefoucault is, I know, blamed, but I think without reason, for deriving all our actions from the source of self-love. For my own part, I see a great deal of truth, and no harm at all, in that opinion.

The reflection which is the most censured in Monsieur de la Rochefoucault's book, as a very ill-natured one, is this: "On trouve dans le malheur de son meilleur ami, quelque chose qui ne déplaît pas." And why not? Why may I not feel a very tender and real concern for the misfortune of my friend, and yet at the same time feel a pleasing consciousness at having discharged my duty to him, by comforting and assisting him to the utmost of my power in that misfortune? Give me but virtuous actions, and I will not quibble and chicane about the motives. And I will give anybody their choice of these two truths, which amount to the same thing: He who loves himself best is the honestest man; or, The honestest man loves himself best. [*Same date.*]

Woman. — As women are a considerable, or at least a pretty numerous part of company, and as their suffrages go a great way toward establishing a man's character, in the fashionable part of the world (which is of great importance to the fortune and figure he proposes to make in it), it is necessary to please them. I will, therefore, upon this subject, let you into certain *arcana* that will be very useful for you to know, but which you must, with the utmost care, conceal; and never seem to know. Women, then, are only children of a larger growth; they have an entertaining tattle, and sometimes wit; but for solid, reasoning good sense, I never in my life knew one that had it, or who reasoned or acted consequentially for four-and-twenty hours together. Some little passion or humor always breaks in upon their best resolutions. Their beauty neglected or controverted, their age increased, or their supposed understandings depreciated, instantly kindles their little passions, and overturns any system of consequential conduct, that in their most reasonable moments they might have been capable of forming. A man of sense only trifles with them, plays with them, humors and flatters them, as he does with a sprightly, forward child; but he neither consults them about, nor trusts them with, serious matters; though he often makes them believe that he does both, which is the thing in the world that they are proud of, for they love mightily to be dabbling in business (which, by the way, they always spoil); and being justly distrustful, that men in general look upon them in a trifling light, they almost adore that man who talks more seriously to them, and who seems to consult and trust them — I say, who seems — for weak men really do, but wise ones only seem to do it. No flattery is either too high or too low for them. They will greedily swallow the highest, and gracefully accept of the lowest; and you may safely flatter any woman, from her understanding down to the exquisite taste of her fan. Women, who are either indisputably beautiful or indisputably ugly, are best flattered upon the score of their understandings; but those who are in a state of mediocrity are best flattered upon their beauty, or at least their graces, for every woman who is not absolutely ugly thinks herself handsome, but not hearing often that she is so, is the more grateful and the more obliged to the few who tell her so; whereas a decided and conscious beauty looks upon every tribute paid to her beauty only as her due, but wants to shine, and to be considered on the side of her understanding; and a woman, who is ugly enough to know that she is so, knows that she has nothing left for it but her understanding, which is consequently, (and probably in more senses than one) her weak side. But these are secrets which you must keep inviolably, if you would not, like Orpheus, be torn to pieces by the whole sex. On the contrary, a man who thinks of living in the great world must be gallant, polite, and attentive to please the women. They have from the weakness of men, more or less influence in all courts; they absolutely stamp every man's character in the *beau monde*, and make it either current, or cry it down, and stop it in payments. It is, therefore, absolutely necessary to manage, please, and flatter them; and never to discover the least marks of contempt, which is what they never forgive; but in this they are not singular, for it is the same with men; who will much sooner forgive an injustice than an insult. [*Same date.*]

Contempt.—Every man is not ambitious, or covetous, or passionate; but every man has pride enough in his composition to feel and resent the least slight and contempt. Remember, therefore, most carefully to conceal your contempt, however just, wherever you would not make an implacable enemy. Men are much more unwilling to have their weaknesses and their imperfections known, than their crimes; and, if you hint to a man that you think him silly, ignorant or even ill-bred or awkward, he will hate you more and longer than if you tell him, plainly, that you think him a rogue. Never yield to that temptation, which, to most young men, is very strong, of exposing other people's weaknesses and infirmities, for the sake either of diverting the company, or of showing your own superiority. You may get the laugh on your side by it, for the present; but you will make enemies by it for ever; and even those who laugh with you then, will, upon reflection, fear, and consequently hate you; besides that, it is ill-natured; and a good heart desires rather to conceal, than expose, other people's weaknesses or misfortunes. If you have wit, use it to please, and not to hurt; you may shine, like the sun in the temperate zones, without scorching. Here it is wished for; under the line it is dreaded. [*Same date.*]

Caligula.—Another very just observation of the Cardinal's36 is, that the things which happen in our own times, and which we see ourselves, do not surprise us near so much as the things which we read of in times past, though not in the least more extraordinary; and adds that he is persuaded that, when Caligula made his horse a consul, the people of Rome at that time were not greatly surprised at it, having necessarily been in some degree prepared for it, by an insensible gradation of extravagancies from the same quarter. [*Sept. 13, 1748.*]

Antiquity is Strange. — We read every day, with astonishment, things which we see every day without surprise. We wonder at the intrepidity of a Leonidas, a Codrus, and a Curtius; and are not the least surprised to hear of a sea captain who has blown up his ship, his crew, and himself, that they might not fall into the hands of the enemies of his country. I cannot help reading of Porsenna and Regulus with surprise and reverence; and yet I remember that I saw, without either, the execution of Shepherd, a boy of eighteen years old, who intended to shoot the late king, and who would have been pardoned if he would have expressed the least sorrow for his intended crime; but, on the contrary, he declared, that, if he was pardoned, he would attempt it again; that he thought it a duty which he owed his country; and that he died with pleasure for having endeavored to perform it. Reason equals Shepherd to Regulus; but prejudice, and the recency of the fact, make Shepherd a common malefactor, and Regulus a hero. [*Same date.*]

Secrets. — The last observation that I shall now mention of the Cardinal's is, "That a secret is more easily kept by a good many people than one commonly imagines." By this he means a secret of importance among people interested in the keeping of it. And it is certain that people of business know the importance of secrecy, and will observe it where they are concerned in the event. To go and tell any friend, wife, or mistress, any secret with which they have nothing to do, is discovering to them such an unretentive weakness as must convince them that you will tell it to twenty others, and consequently that they may reveal it without the risk of being discovered. But a secret properly communicated only to those who are to be concerned in the thing in question, will probably be kept by them, though they should be a good many. Little secrets are commonly told again, but great ones generally kept. Adieu. [*Same date.*]

Trifles. — How trifling soever these things may seem, or really be, in themselves, they are no longer so, when above half the world thinks them otherwise. And, as I would have you *omnibus ornatum — excellere rebus*, I think nothing above or below my pointing out to you, or your excelling in. You have the means of doing it, and time before you to make use of them. Take my word for it, I ask nothing now but what you will, twenty years hence, most heartily wish that you had done. [*Sept. 20, 1748.*]

The Pedant and the Scholar. — A gentleman has, probably, read no other Latin than that of the Augustan age; and therefore can write no other; whereas the pedant has read much more bad Latin than good; and consequently writes so too. He looks upon the best classical books as books for schoolboys, and consequently below him, but pores over fragments of obscure authors, treasures up the obsolete words which he meets with there, and uses them upon all occasions, to show his reading at the expense of his judgment. Plautus is his favorite author, not for the sake of the wit and the *vis comica* of his comedies; but upon account of the many obsolete words and the cant of low characters, which are to be met with nowhere else. He will rather use *olli* than *illi*, *optumè* than *optimè*, and any bad word, rather than any good one, provided he can but prove that, strictly speaking, it is Latin; that is, that it was written by a Roman. [*Sept. 27, 1748.*]

A Detestable Doctrine. — I must now say something as to the matter of the lecture; in which I confess there is one doctrine laid down that surprises me; it is this: "Quum vero hostis sit lenta citave morte omnia dira nobis minitans quocunque bellantibus negotium est, parum sane interfuerit quo modo eum obruere et interficere satagamus si ferociam exuere cunctetur. Ergo veneno quoque uti fas est," etc., whereas I cannot conceive that the use of poison can, upon any account, come within the lawful means of self-defence. Force may, without doubt, be justly repelled by force; but not by treachery and fraud; for I do not call the stratagems of war, such as ambuscades, masked batteries, false attacks, etc., frauds or treachery; they are mutually to be expected and guarded against; but poisoned arrows, poisoned waters, or poison administered to your enemy (which can only be done by treachery), I have always heard, read, and thought to be unlawful and infamous means of defence, be your danger ever so great; but, *si ferociam exuere cunctetur;* must I rather die than poison this enemy? Yes, certainly, much rather die than do a base or criminal action; nor can I be sure, beforehand, that this enemy may not in the last moment *ferociam exuere.* But the public lawyers now seem to me rather to warp the law, in order to authorize than to check those unlawful proceedings of princes and states; which, by being become common, appear less criminal; though custom can never alter the nature of good and ill.

Pray let no quibbles of lawyers, no refinements of casuists break into the plain notions of right and wrong which every man's right reason and plain common sense suggest to him. To do as you would be done by is the plain, sure, and undisputed rule of morality and justice. Stick to that; and be convinced that whatever breaks into it, in any degree, however speciously it may be turned, and however puzzling it may be to answer it, is, notwithstanding, false in itself, unjust, and criminal. I do not know a crime in the world which is not, by the casuists among the Jesuits (especially the twenty-four collected, I think, by Escobar) allowed in some, or many cases, not to be criminal. The principles first laid down by them are often specious, the reasonings plausible; but the conclusion always a lie; for it is contrary to that evident and undeniable rule of justice which I have mentioned above, of not doing to any one what you would not have him do to you. But, however, these refined pieces of casuistry and sophistry being very convenient and welcome to people's passions and appetites, they gladly accept the indulgence without desiring to detect the fallacy of the reasoning; and indeed many, I might say most people, are not able to do it; which makes the publication of such quibblings and refinements the more pernicious. I am no skilful casuist nor subtle disputant; and yet I would undertake to justify and qualify the profession of a highwayman step by step, and so plausibly as to make many ignorant people embrace the profession as an innocent, if not even a laudable one; and to puzzle people of some degree of knowledge to answer me point by point. I have seen a book entitled "Quidlibet ex Quolibet," or the art of making any thing out of any thing; which is not so difficult as it would seem, if once one quits certain plain truths, obvious in growth to every understanding, in order to run after the ingenious refinements of warm imaginations and speculative reasonings. Doctor Berkeley, Bishop of Cloyne, a very worthy, ingenious, and learned man, has written a book to prove that there is no such thing as matter, and that nothing exists but in idea; that you and I only fancy ourselves eating, drinking, and sleeping; you at Leipsic, and I at London; that we think we have flesh and blood, legs, arms, etc., but that we are only spirit. His arguments are, strictly speaking, unanswerable; but yet I am so far from being convinced by them that I am determined to go on to eat and drink, and walk and ride, in order to keep that *matter*, which I so mistakenly imagine my body at present to consist of, in as good plight as possible. Common sense (which, in truth, is very uncommon) is the best sense I know of; abide by it; it will counsel you best. Read and hear for your amusement, ingenious systems, nice questions, subtlely agitated, with all the refinements that warm imaginations suggest; but consider them only as exercitations for the mind, and return always to settle with common sense. [*Same date.*]

Letters.—Your letters, except when upon a given subject, are exceedingly laconic, and neither answer my desires, nor the purpose of letters; which should be familiar conversations, between absent friends. As I desire to live with you upon the footing of an intimate friend, and not of a parent, I could wish that your letters gave me more particular accounts of yourself, and of your lesser transactions. When you write to me, suppose yourself conversing freely with me, by the fireside. In that case, you would naturally mention the incidents of the day; as where you had been, whom you had seen, what you thought of them, etc. Do this in your letters; acquaint me sometimes with your studies, sometimes with your diversions; tell me of any new persons and characters that you meet with in company, and add your own observations upon them; in short, let me see more of you, in your letters. [*Same date.*]

Good Company. — To keep good company, especially at your first setting out, is the way to receive good impressions. If you ask me what I mean by good company, I will confess to you that it is pretty difficult to define; but I will endeavor to make you understand it as well as I can.

Good company is not what respective sets of company are pleased either to call or think themselves; but it is that company which all the people of the place call, and acknowledge to be good company, notwithstanding some objections which they may form to some of the individuals who compose it. It consists chiefly (but by no means without exception) of people of considerable birth, rank, and character: for people of neither birth nor rank are frequently and very justly admitted into it, if distinguished by any peculiar merit, or eminency in any liberal art or science. Nay, so motley a thing is good company, that many people without birth, rank, or merit, intrude into it by their own forwardness; and others slide into it by the protection of some considerable person; and some even of indifferent characters and morals make part of it. But, in the main, the good part preponderates, and people of infamous and blasted characters are never admitted. In this fashionable good company the best manners and the best language of the place are most unquestionably to be learnt; for they establish and give the tone to both, which are therefore called the language and manners of good company; there being no legal tribunal to ascertain either.

A company consisting wholly of people of the first quality cannot, for that reason, be called good company, in the common acceptation of the phrase, unless they are, into the bargain, the fashionable and accredited company of the place; for people of the very first quality can be as silly, as ill-bred, and as worthless, as people of the meanest degree. On the other hand, a company consisting entirely of people of very low condition, whatever their merits or parts may be, can never be called good company; and consequently, should not be much frequented, though by no means despised.

A company wholly composed of men of learning, though greatly to be valued and respected, is not meant by the words *good company*: they cannot have the easy manners and *tournure* of the world, as they do not live in it. If you can bear your part well in such a company, it is extremely right to be in it sometimes, and you will be but more esteemed, in other companies, for having a place in that. But then do not let it engross you; for if you do, you will be only considered as one of the *litterati* by profession; which is not the way either to shine or rise in the world.

The company of professed wits and poets is extremely inviting to most young men; who, if they have wit themselves, are pleased with it, and if they have none, are sillily proud of being one of it: but it should be frequented with moderation and judgment, and you should by no means give yourself up to it. A wit is a very unpopular denomination, as it carries terror along with it; and people in general are as much afraid of a live wit, in company, as a woman is of a gun, which she thinks may go off of itself, and do her a mischief. Their acquaintance is, however, worth seeking, and their company worth frequenting; but not exclusively of others, nor to such a degree as to be considered only as one of that particular set.

But the company, which of all others you should most carefully avoid, is that low company, which in every sense of the word, is low indeed; low in rank, low in parts, low in manners, and low in merit [*Oct. 12, 1748.*]

Associates. — There is good sense in the Spanish saying, "Tell me whom you live with, and I will tell you who you are." Make it therefore your business, wherever you are, to get into that company which everybody of the place allows to be the best company, next to their own: which is the best definition that I can give you of good company. But here, too, one caution is very necessary; for want of which many young men have been ruined, even in good company. Good company (as I have before observed) is composed of a great variety of fashionable people, whose characters and morals are very different, though their manners are pretty much the same. When a young man, now in the world, first gets into that company, he very rightly determines to conform to and imitate it. But then he too often, and fatally, mistakes the objects of his imitation. He has often heard that absurd term of genteel and fashionable vices. [*Same date.*]

Behavior. — Imitate, then, with discernment and judgment, the real perfections of the good company into which you may get; copy their politeness, their carriage, their address, and the easy and well-bred turn of their conversation; but remember that, let them shine ever so bright, their vices, if they have any, are so many spots which you would no more imitate than you would make an artificial wart upon your face, because some very handsome man had the misfortune to have a natural one upon his; but, on the contrary, think how much handsomer he would have been without it. [*Same date.*]

Talking. — Talk often, but never long; in that case, if you do not please, at least you are sure not to tire your hearers. Pay your own reckoning, but do not treat the whole company; this being one of the very few cases in which people do not care to be treated, every one being fully convinced that he has wherewithal to pay.

Tell stories seldom, and absolutely never but where they are very apt and very short. Omit every circumstance that is not material, and beware of digressions. To have frequent recourse to narrative betrays great want of imagination.

Never hold anybody by the button or the hand, in order to be heard out; for if people are not willing to hear you, you had much better hold your tongue than them.

Most long talkers single out some one unfortunate man in company (commonly him whom they observe to be the most silent, or their next neighbor) to whisper, or at least, in a half voice, to convey a continuity of words to. This is excessively ill-bred, and, in some degree, a fraud; conversation stock being a joint and common property. But, on the other hand, if one of these unmerciful talkers lays hold of you, hear him with patience (and at least seeming attention) if he is worth obliging; for nothing will oblige him more than a patient hearing, as nothing would hurt him more than either to leave him in the midst of his discourse or to discover your impatience under your affliction.

Take rather than give the tone of the company you are in. If you have parts you will show them more or less upon every subject; and if you have not, you had better talk sillily upon a subject of other people's than of your own choosing.

Avoid as much as you can in mixed companies, argumentative, polemical conversations; which, though they should not, yet certainly do, indispose, for a time, the contending parties towards each other; and if the controversy grows warm and noisy, endeavor to put an end to it by some genteel levity or joke. I quieted such a conversation hubbub once by presenting to them that, though I was persuaded none there present would repeat out of company what passed in it, yet I could not answer for the discretion of the passengers in the street, who must necessarily hear all that was said.

Above all things, and upon all occasions, avoid speaking of yourself if it be possible. Such is the natural pride and vanity of our hearts that it perpetually breaks out, even in people of the best parts, in all the various modes and figures of the egotism. [*Oct. 19, 1748.*]

Silly Vanity.—This principle of vanity and pride is so strong in human nature that it descends even to the lowest objects; and one often sees people angling for praise, where, admitting all they say to be true (which, by the way, it seldom is), no just praise is to be caught. One man affirms that he has rode post a hundred miles in six hours; probably it is a lie; but supposing it to be true, what then? Why, he is a very good postboy, that is all. Another asserts, and probably not without oaths, that he has drunk six or eight bottles of wine at a sitting; out of charity I will believe him a liar; for if I do not, I must think him a beast. [*Same date.*]

Yourself. — The only sure way of avoiding these evils is never to speak of yourself at all. But when historically you are obliged to mention yourself, take care not to drop one single word that can directly or indirectly be construed as fishing for applause. Be your character what it will, it will be known; and nobody will take it upon your own word. Never imagine that anything you can say yourself will varnish your defects or add lustre to your perfections; but on the contrary, it may, and nine times in ten will, make the former more glaring and the latter obscure. If you are silent upon your own subject, neither envy, indignation, nor ridicule will obstruct or allay the applause which you may really deserve; but if you publish your own panegyric upon any occasion or in any shape whatsoever, and however artfully dressed or disguised, they will all conspire against you, and you will be disappointed of the very end you aim at. [*Same date.*]

Scandal — Mimicry — Swearing — Laughter. — Neither retail nor receive scandal willingly; for though the defamation of others may for the present gratify the malignity of the pride of our hearts, cool reflection will draw very disadvantageous conclusions from such a disposition; and in the case of scandal, as in that of robbery, the receiver is always thought as bad as the thief.

Mimicry, which is the common and favorite amusement of little, low minds, is in the utmost contempt with great ones. It is the lowest and most illiberal of all buffoonery. Pray neither practise it yourself, nor applaud it in others. Besides that, the person mimicked is insulted; and as I have often observed to you before, an insult is never forgiven.

I need not (I believe) advise you to adapt your conversation to the people you are conversing with; for I suppose you would not, without this caution, have talked upon the same subject and in the same manner to a minister of state, a bishop, a philosopher, a captain, and a woman. A man of the world must, like the chameleon (*sic*), be able to take every different hue; which is by no means a criminal or abject, but a necessary complaisance, for it relates only to manners, and not to morals.

One word only as to swearing; and that I hope and believe is more than is necessary. You may sometimes hear some people in good company interlard their discourse with oaths by way of embellishment, as they think; but you must observe, too, that those who do so are never those who contribute in any degree to give that company the denomination of good company. They are always subalterns or people of low education; for that practice, besides that it has no one temptation to plead, is as silly and as illiberal as it is wicked.

Loud laughter is the mirth of the mob, who are only pleased with silly things; for true wit or good sense never excited a laugh since the creation of the world. A man of parts and fashion is therefore only seen to smile, but never heard to laugh.

But to conclude this long letter; all the above-mentioned rules, however carefully you may observe them, will lose half their effect if unaccompanied by the Graces. Whatever you say, if you say it with a supercilious, cynical face, or an embarrassed countenance, or a silly, disconcerted grin, will be ill received. If, into the bargain, *you mutter it, or utter it indistinctly and ungracefully*, it will be still worse received. If your air and address are vulgar, awkward, and *gauche*, you may be esteemed indeed, if you have great intrinsic merit; but you will never please, and, without pleasing, you will rise but heavily. Venus, among the ancients, was synonymous with the Graces, who were always supposed to accompany her; and Horace tells us that even Youth and Mercury, the god of arts and eloquence, would not do without her.

" —Paràm comis *sine te Juventas,*

Mercuriusque."

They are not inexorable ladies, and may be had if properly and diligently pursued. Adieu. [*Same date.*]

The Duty of a Mentor. —I have long since done mentioning your great religious and moral duties; because I could not make your understanding so bad a compliment, as to suppose that you wanted, or could receive, any new instructions upon those two important points. Mr. Harte, I am sure, has not neglected them; besides, they are so obvious to common sense and reason, that commentators may (as they often do) perplex, but cannot make them clearer. My province, therefore, is to supply, by my experience, your, hitherto, inevitable inexperience in the ways of the world. People at your age are in a state of natural ebriety; and want rails, and *gardefous*, wherever they go, to hinder them from breaking their necks. This drunkenness of youth is not only tolerated, but even pleases, if kept within certain bounds of discretion and decency. Those bounds are the point which it is difficult for the drunken man himself to find out; and there it is that the experience of a friend may not only serve but save him.

Carry with you, and welcome, into company, all the gaiety and spirits, but as little of the giddiness, of youth as you can. The former will charm; but the latter will often, though innocently, implacably offend. Inform yourself of the characters and situations of the company, before you give way to what your imagination may prompt you to say. There are, in all companies, more wrong heads than right ones, and many more who deserve than who like censure. [*Oct. 29, 1748.*]

Egotism.—Cautiously avoid talking of either your own or other people's domestic affairs.37 Yours are nothing to them, but tedious; theirs are nothing to you. The subject is a tender one; and it is odds but you touch somebody or other's sore place; for, in this case, there is no trusting to specious appearances; which may be, and often are, so contrary to the real situation of things, between men and their wives, parents and their children, seeming friends, etc., that, with the best intentions in the world, one often blunders disagreeably.

Remember, that the wit, humor, and jokes of most mixed companies are local. They thrive in that particular soil, but will not often bear transplanting. Every company is differently circumstanced, has its particular cant, and jargon; which may give occasion to wit and mirth, within that circle, but would seem flat and insipid in any other, and therefore will not bear repeating. [*Same date.*]

Good Fellows.—You will find, in most good company, some people who only keep their place there by a contemptible title enough; these are what we call *very good-natured fellows*, and the French *bons diables*. The truth is, they are people without any parts or fancy, and who, having no will of their own, readily assent to, concur in, and applaud, whatever is said or done in the company; and adopt, with the same alacrity, the most virtuous or the most criminal, the wisest or the silliest scheme, that happens to be entertained by the majority of the company. This foolish, and often criminal, complaisance flows from a foolish cause; the want of any other merit. I hope you will hold your place in company by a nobler tenure, and that you will hold it (you can bear a quibble, I believe, yet) *in capite*. Have a will and an opinion of your own, and adhere to them steadily; but then do it with good humor, good breeding, and (if you have it) with urbanity; for you have not yet beard enough either to preach or censure. [*Same date.*]

The Fine Gentleman.—What the French justly call *les manières nobles*, are only to be acquired in the very best companies. They are the distinguishing characteristics of men of fashion: people of low education never wear them so close, but that some part or other of the original vulgarism appears. *Les manières nobles* equally forbid insolent contempt, or low envy and jealousy. Low people, in good circumstances, fine clothes, and equipage, will insolently show contempt for all those who cannot afford as fine clothes, as good an equipage, and who have not (as they term it) as much money in their pockets: on the other hand, they are gnawed with envy, and cannot help discovering it, of those who surpass them in any of these articles; which are far from being sure criterions of merit. They are, likewise, jealous of being slighted; and, consequently, suspicious and captious: they are eager and hot about trifles; because trifles were, at first, their affairs of consequence. *Les manières nobles* imply exactly the reverse of all this. Study them early; you cannot make them too habitual and familiar to you. [*Same date.*]

I like the description of your *pic-nic*;38 where, I take it for granted, that your cards are only to break the formality of a circle, and your symposium intended more to promote conversation than drinking. Such an *amicable collision*, as Lord Shaftesbury very prettily calls it, rubs off and smooths those rough corners, which mere nature has given to the smoothest of us. I hope some part, at least, of the conversation is in German. [*Same date.*]

The Graces.—I send you Mr. Locke's book upon education, in which you will find the stress he lays upon the graces, which he calls (and very truly) good breeding. I have marked all the parts of that book which are worth your attention; for as he begins with the child, almost from its birth, the parts relative to its infancy would be useless to you. Germany is, still less than England, the seat of the graces; however you had as good not to say so while you are there. [*Nov. 18, 1748.*]

The Duke of Marlborough.—Of all the men that ever I knew in my life (and I knew him extremely well), the late Duke of Marlborough possessed the graces in the highest degree, not to say engrossed them; and indeed he got the most by them; for I will venture (contrary to the custom of profound historians, who always assign deep causes for great events) to ascribe the better half of the Duke of Marlborough's greatness and riches to those graces. He was eminently illiterate; wrote bad English, and spelled it still worse. He had no share of what is commonly called *parts*; that is, he had no brightness, nothing shining in his genius. He had, most undoubtedly, an excellent good plain understanding, with sound judgment. But these alone would probably have raised him but something higher than they found him; which was page to King James the Second's Queen. There the graces protected and promoted him; for, while he was an ensign of the Guards, the Duchess of Cleveland, then favorite mistress to King Charles the Second, struck by those very graces, gave him five thousand pounds, with which he immediately bought an annuity for his life, of five hundred pounds a year, of my grandfather, Halifax, which was the foundation of his subsequent fortune. His figure was beautiful, but his manner was irresistible, to either man or woman. It was by this engaging, graceful manner that he was enabled, during all his war, to connect the various and jarring powers of the Grand Alliance, and to carry them on to the main object of the war, notwithstanding their private and separate views, jealousies, and wrongheadedness. Whatever court he went to (and he was often obliged to go himself to some testy and refractory ones), he as constantly prevailed, and brought them into his measures. The Pensionary Heinsius, a venerable old minister, grown gray in business, and who had governed the Republic of the United Provinces for more than forty years, was absolutely governed by the Duke of Marlborough, as that republic feels to this day. He was always cool; and nobody ever observed the least variation in his countenance; he could refuse more gracefully than other people could grant; and those who went away from him the most dissatisfied, as to the substance of their business, were yet personally charmed with him, and, in some degree, comforted by his manner. With all his gentleness and gracefulness, no man living was more conscious of his situation, nor maintained his dignity better. [*Same date.*]

A Father's Anxiety. — This subject is inexhaustible, as it extends to everything that is to be said or done; but I will leave it for the present, as this letter is already pretty long. Such is my desire, my anxiety for your perfection, that I never think I have said enough, though you may possibly think I have said too much; and though, in truth, if your own good sense is not sufficient to direct you, in many of these plain points, all that I or anybody else can say will be insufficient. But, where you are concerned, I am the insatiable man in Horace, who covets still a little corner more, to complete the figure of his field. I dread every little corner that may deform mine, in which I would have (if possible) no one defect. [*Same date.*]

Mourning. — I am at present under very great concern for the loss of a most affectionate brother, with whom I had always lived in the closest friendship. My brother John died last Friday night, of a fit of the gout, which he had had for about a month in his hands and feet, and which fell at last upon his stomach and head. As he grew, towards the last, lethargic, his end was not painful to himself. At the distance which you are from hence, you need not go into mourning upon this occasion, as the time of your mourning would be near over before you could put it on. [*Dec. 6, 1748.*]

Frivolity. — Little minds mistake little objects for great ones, and lavish away upon the former that time and attention which only the latter deserve. To such mistakes we owe the numerous and frivolous tribe of insect-mongers, shell-mongers, and pursuers and driers of butterflies, etc. The strong mind distinguishes, not only between the useful and the useless, but likewise between the useful and the curious. He applies himself intensely to the former; he only amuses himself with the latter. Of this little sort of knowledge, which I have just hinted at, you will find, at least, as much as you need wish to know, in a superficial but pretty French book, entitled "Spectacle de la Nature," which will amuse you while you read it, and give you a sufficient notion of the various parts of nature; I would advise you to read it at leisure hours. [*Same date.*]

Astronomy.—But that part of nature which, Mr. Harte tells me, you have begun to study, with the *Rector magnificus*, is of much greater importance, and deserves much more attention; I mean astronomy. The vast and immense planetary system, the astonishing order and regularity of those innumerable worlds, will open a scene to you which not only deserves your attention as a matter of curiosity, or rather astonishment; but, still more, as it will give you greater and consequently juster ideas of that eternal and omnipotent Being, who contrived, made, and still preserves that universe, than all the contemplation of this, comparatively, very little orb, which we at present inhabit, could possibly give you. Upon this subject, Monsieur Fontenelle's "Pluralité des Mondes," which you may read in two hours' time, will both inform and please you. God bless you! Yours. [*Same date.*]

The whole morning, if diligently and attentively devoted to solid studies, will go a great way at the year's end; and the evenings spent in the pleasures of good company will go as far in teaching you a knowledge not much less necessary than the other—I mean the knowledge of the world. Between these two necessary studies, that of books in the morning, and that of the world in the evening, you see that you will not have one minute to squander or slattern away. Nobody ever lent themselves more than I did, when I was young, to the pleasures and dissipation of good company; I even did it too much. But then, I can assure you that I always found time for serious studies; and when I could find it no other way, I took it out of my sleep, for I resolved always to rise early in the morning, however late I went to bed at night; and this resolution I have kept so sacred that, unless when I have been confined to my bed by illness, I have not for more than forty years ever been in bed at nine o'clock in the morning, but commonly up before eight. [*Dec. 13, 1748.*]

Writing.—Why do you not form your Roman characters better? for I maintain that it is in every man's power to write what hand he pleases; and consequently that he ought to write a good one. You form, particularly, your ee and your ll in zigzag, instead of making them straight, as thus, *ee, ll*; a fault very easily mended. You will not, I believe, be angry with this little criticism, when I tell you that, by all the accounts I have had of late, from Mr. Harte and others, this is the only criticism that you give me occasion to make. [*Dec. 20, 1748.*]

A Portrait.—Consider what lustre and *éclat* it will give you when you return here, to be allowed to be the best scholar, of a gentleman, in England; not to mention the real pleasure and solid comfort which such knowledge will give you throughout your whole life. Mr. Harte tells me another thing which, I own, I did not expect; it is that, when you read aloud, or repeat part of plays, you speak very properly and distinctly. This relieves me from great uneasiness, which I was under upon account of your former bad enunciation. Go on, and attend most diligently to this important article. It is, of all the graces (and they are all necessary), the most necessary one. [*Same date.*]

The Desire of Praise.—But here let me, as an old stager upon the theatre of the world, suggest one consideration to you, which is, to extend your desire of praise a little beyond the strictly praiseworthy; or else you may be apt to discover too much contempt for at least three parts in the five of the world, who will never forgive it you. In the mass of mankind, I fear, there is too great a majority of fools and knaves; who, singly from their number, must to a certain degree be respected, though they are by no means respectable. And a man, who will show every knave or fool that he thinks him such, will engage in a most ruinous war, against numbers much superior to those that he and his allies can bring into the field. Abhor a knave, and pity a fool in your heart, but let neither of them, unnecessarily, see that you do so. Some complaisance and attention to fools is prudent, and not mean; as a silent abhorrence of individual knaves is often necessary, and not criminal. [*Same date.*]

A Compliment.—Lady Chesterfield bids me tell you that she decides entirely in your favor,39 against Mr. Grevenkop, and even against herself; for she does not think that she could, at this time, write either so good a character, or so good German. Pray write her a German letter upon that subject; in which you may tell her that, like the rest of the world, you approve of her judgment, because it is in your favor; and that you true Germans cannot allow Danes to be competent judges of your language, etc. [*Same date.*]

Affectation. — Any affectation whatsoever in dress implies, in my mind, a flaw in the understanding. Most of our young fellows here display some character or other by their dress: some affect the tremendous, and wear a great and fiercely cocked hat, an enormous sword, a short waistcoat, and a black cravat; these I should be almost tempted to swear the peace against, in my own defence, if I were not convinced that they are but meek asses in lions' skins. Others go in brown frocks, leather breeches, great oaken cudgels in their hands, their hats uncocked, and their hair unpowdered; and imitate grooms, stage-coachmen, and country bumpkins, so well in their outsides, that I do not make the least doubt of their resembling them equally in their insides. A man of sense carefully avoids any particular character in his dress; he is accurately clean for his own sake; but all the rest is for other people's. He dresses as well, and in the same manner, as the people of sense and fashion of the place where he is. If he dresses better, as he thinks, that is, more than they, he is a fop; if he dresses worse, he is unpardonably negligent; but, of the two, I would rather have a young fellow too much than too little dressed; the excess on that side will wear off, with a little age and reflection; but if he is negligent at twenty, he will be a sloven at forty, and stink at fifty years old. Dress yourself fine, where others are fine; and plain, where others are plain; but take care, always, that your clothes are well made and fit you, for otherwise they will give you a very awkward air. When you are once well dressed for the day, think no more of it afterwards; and, without any stiffness for fear of discomposing that dress, let all your motions be as easy and natural as if you had no clothes on at all. So much for dress, which I maintain to be a thing of consequence in the polite world. [*Dec. 30, 1748.*]

A Happy New Year. — I send you, my dear child (and you will not doubt), very sincerely, the wishes of the season. May you deserve a great number of happy new years; and, if you deserve, may you have them! Many new years, indeed, you may see, but happy ones you cannot see without deserving them. These, virtue, honor, and knowledge, alone can merit, alone can procure. "Dii tibi dent annos de te nam cætera sumes," was a pretty piece of poetical flattery, where it was said; I hope that in time it may be no flattery when said to you. But, I assure you, that, whenever I cannot apply the latter part of the line to you with truth, I shall neither say, think, nor wish the former. Adieu. [*Same date.*]

Rational Pleasures. — Now that you are going a little more into the world, I will take this occasion to explain my intentions as to your future expenses, that you may know what you have to expect from me, and make your plan accordingly. I shall neither deny nor grudge you any money that may be necessary for either your improvement or your pleasures; I mean, the pleasures of a rational being. Under the head of improvement, I mean the best books, and the best masters, cost what they will; I also mean all the expense of lodgings, coach, dress, servants, etc., which, according to the several places where you may be, shall be respectively necessary, to enable you to keep the best company. Under the head of rational pleasures, I comprehend, first, proper charities, to real and compassionate objects of it; secondly, proper presents, to those to whom you are obliged, or whom you desire to oblige; thirdly, a conformity of expense to that of the company which you keep — as in public spectacles, your share of little entertainments, a few pistoles at games of mere commerce, and other incidental calls of good company. The only two articles which I will never supply, are the profusion of low riot and the idle lavishness of negligence and laziness. A fool squanders away, without credit or advantage to himself, more than a man of sense spends with both. The latter employs his money as he does his time, and neither spends a shilling of the one, nor a minute of the other, but in something that is either useful or rationally pleasing to himself or others. The former buys whatever he does not want, and does not pay for what he does want. He cannot withstand the charms of a toy-shop; snuff-boxes, watches, heads of canes, etc., are his destruction. His servants and tradesmen conspire with his own indolence, to cheat him; and, in a little time, he is astonished, in the midst of all the ridiculous superfluities, to find himself in want of all the real comforts and necessaries of life. Without care and method the largest fortune will not, and with them, almost the smallest will, supply all necessary expenses. As far as you can possibly, pay ready money for everything you buy, and avoid bills. Pay that money too, yourself, and not through the hands of any servant, who always either stipulates poundage, or requires a present for his good word, as they call it. Where you must have bills (as for meat and drink, clothes, etc.) pay them regularly every month, and with your own hand. Never, from a mistaken economy, buy a thing you do not want, because it is cheap; or, from a silly pride, because it is dear. Keep an account, in a book, of all that you receive, and of all that you pay; for no man, who knows what he receives, and what he pays, ever runs out. I do not mean that you should keep an account of the shillings and half-crowns which you may spend in chair-hire, operas, etc., they are unworthy of the time, and of the ink, that they would consume; leave such *minutiæ* to dull, pennywise fellows; but remember, in economy, as well as in every other part of life, to have the proper attention to proper objects, and the proper contempt for little ones. A strong mind sees things in their true proportions: a weak one views them through a magnifying medium; which, like the microscope, makes an elephant of a flea; magnifies all little objects, but cannot receive great ones. I have known many a man pass for a miser, by saving a penny, and wrangling for two pence, who was undoing himself, at the same time, by living above his income, and not attending to essential articles, which were above his *portée*. The sure characteristic of a sound and strong mind is, to find, in everything, those certain bounds, *quos ultra citrave nequit consistere rectum*. These boundaries are marked out by a very fine line, which only good sense and attention can discover; it is much too fine for vulgar eyes. In manners, this line is good breeding; beyond it, is troublesome ceremony; short of it, is unbecoming negligence and inattention. In morals, it divides ostentatious Puritanism from criminal relaxation; in religion, superstition from impiety; and, in short, every virtue from its kindred vice or weakness. I think you have sense enough to discover the line; keep it always in your eye, and learn to walk upon it; rest upon Mr. Harte, and he will poise you till you are able to go alone. By the way, there are fewer people who walk well upon that line, than upon the slack rope; and therefore a good performer shines so much the more. [*Jan. 10, 1749.*]

Dancing. — Remember to take the best dancing master at Berlin, more to teach you to sit, stand, and walk gracefully, than to dance finely. The Graces, the Graces; remember the Graces! Adieu. [*Same date.*]

The Classics — their Value. — My first prejudice (for I do not mention the prejudices of boys and women, such as hobgoblins, ghosts, dreams, spilling salt, etc.) was my classical enthusiasm, which I received from the books I read, and the masters who explained them to me. I was convinced there had been no common sense nor common honesty in the world for these last fifteen hundred years; but that they were totally extinguished with the ancient Greek and Roman governments. Homer and Virgil could have no faults, because they were ancient; Milton and Tasso could have no merit, because they were modern. And I could almost have said, with regard to the ancients, what Cicero, very absurdly and unbecomingly for a philosopher, says with regard to Plato, "Cum quo errare malim; quam cum aliis rectè sentire." Whereas now, without any extraordinary effort of genius, I have discovered that nature was the same three thousand years ago as it is at present; that men were but men then as well as now; that modes and customs vary often, but that human nature is always the same. And I can no more suppose, that men were better, braver, or wiser, fifteen hundred or three thousand years ago, than I can suppose that the animals or vegetables were better then than they are now. I dare assert too, in defiance of the favorers of the ancients, that Homer's hero, Achilles, was both a brute and a scoundrel, and consequently an improper character for the hero of an epic poem; he had so little regard for his country, that he would not act in defence of it, because he had quarrelled with Agamemnon about a w — — e; and then afterward, animated by private resentment only, he went about killing people basely, I will call it, because he knew himself invulnerable; and yet, invulnerable as he was, he wore the strongest armor in the world; which I humbly apprehend to be a blunder; for a horseshoe clapped to his vulnerable heel would have been sufficient. On the other hand, with submission to the favorers of the moderns, I assert with Mr. Dryden, that the Devil is in truth the hero of Milton's poem: his plan, which he lays, pursues, and at last executes, being the subject of the poem. From all which considerations, I impartially conclude, that the ancients had their excellencies and their defects, their virtues and their vices, just like the moderns: pedantry and affectation of learning decide clearly in favor of the former; vanity and ignorance, as peremptorily, in favor of the latter. Religious prejudices kept pace with my classical ones; and there was a time when I thought it impossible for the honestest man in the world to be saved, out of the pale of the Church of England: not considering that matters of opinion do not depend upon the will; and that it is as natural, and as allowable, that another man should differ in opinion from me, as that I should differ from him; and that, if we are both sincere, we are both blameless: and should consequently have mutual indulgence for each other. [*Feb. 7, 1749.*]

Reflection—its Use.—Use and assert your own reason; reflect, examine, and analyze everything, in order to form a sound and mature judgment; let no ουτος ἔφα impose upon your understanding, mislead your actions, or dictate your conversation. Be early, what, if you are not, you will, when too late, wish you had been. Consult your reason betimes: I do not say that it will always prove an unerring guide; for human reason is not infallible: but it will prove the least erring guide that you can follow. Books and conversation may assist it; but adopt neither, blindly and implicitly; try both by that best rule which God has given to direct us, Reason. Of all the troubles do not decline, as many people do, that of thinking. The herd of mankind can hardly be said to think; their notions are almost all adoptive; and, in general, I believe it is better that it should be so; as such common prejudices contribute more to order and quiet, than their own separate reasonings would do, uncultivated and unimproved as they are. We have many of those useful prejudices in this country, which I should be very sorry to see removed. The good Protestant conviction, that the Pope is both Antichrist, and the Whore of Babylon, is a more effectual preservative, in this country, against popery, than all the solid and unanswerable arguments of Chillingworth.

The idle story of the Pretender's having been introduced in a warming-pan, into the queen's bed, though as destitute of all probability as of all foundation, has been much more prejudicial to the cause of Jacobitism, than all that Mr. Locke and others have written, to show the unreasonableness and absurdity of the doctrines of indefeasible hereditary right and unlimited passive obedience. And that silly, sanguine notion, which is firmly entertained here, that one Englishman can beat three Frenchmen, encourages, and has sometimes enabled one Englishman, in reality, to beat two. [*Same date.*]

Liberty of the Press.—Can an author with reason complain that he is cramped and shackled if he is not at liberty to publish blasphemy, bawdry, or sedition? all which are equally prohibited in the freest governments, if they are wise and well regulated ones. This is the present general complaint of the French authors; but, indeed, chiefly of the bad ones. No wonder, say they, that England produces so many great geniuses; people there may think as they please, and publish what they think. Very true, but who hinders them from thinking as they please? If, indeed, they think in a manner destructive of all religion, morality, or good manners, or to the disturbance of the state; an absolute government will certainly more effectually prohibit them from, or punish them for publishing such thoughts, than a free one could do. But how does that cramp the genius of an epic, dramatic, or lyric poet? Or how does it corrupt the eloquence of an orator, in the pulpit or at the bar? [*Same date.*]

Graceful Behavior. — There is another object that must keep pace with and accompany knowledge; I mean, manners, politeness, and the graces; in which Sir Charles Williams, though very much your friend, owns you are very deficient. The manners of Leipsic must be shook off; and in that respect you must put on the new man. No scrambling at your meals, as at a German ordinary; no awkward overturns of glasses, plates, and salt-cellars; no horse-play. On the contrary, a gentleness of manners, a graceful carriage, and an insinuating address, must take their place. I repeat, and shall never cease repeating to you, *the Graces, the Graces.* [*April 12, 1749.*]

A Gentleman's Pleasures. — Dear Boy: This letter will, I believe, still find you at Venice, in all the dissipation of masquerades, ridottos, operas, etc.: with all my heart; they are decent evening amusements, and very properly succeed that serious application to which I am sure you devote your mornings. There are liberal and illiberal pleasures, as well as liberal and illiberal arts. There are some pleasures, that degrade a gentleman, as much as some trades could do. Sottish drinking, indiscriminate gluttony, driving coaches, rustic sports, such as fox-chases, horse-races, etc., are, in my opinion, infinitely below the honest and industrious professions of a tailor, and a shoemaker, which are said to *déroger.* [*April 19, 1749.*]

Music — Fiddling. — I cannot help cautioning you against giving into those (I will call them illiberal) pleasures (though music is commonly reckoned one of the liberal arts) to the degree that most of your countrymen do when they travel in Italy. If you love music, hear it; go to operas, concerts, and pay fiddlers to play to you; but I insist upon your neither piping nor fiddling yourself. It puts a gentleman in a very frivolous, contemptible light; brings him into a great deal of bad company; and takes up a great deal of time, which might be much better employed. Few things would mortify me more than to see you bearing a part in a concert, with a fiddle under your chin, or a pipe in your mouth. [*Same date.*]

Manières. — By *manières*, I do not mean bare common civility; everybody must have that, who would not be kicked out of company; but I mean engaging, insinuating, shining manners; a distinguished politeness, an almost irresistible address; a superior gracefulness in all you say and do.

It is this alone that can give all your other talents their full lustre and value; and consequently, it is this which should now be the principal object of your attention. Observe minutely, wherever you go, the allowed and established morals of good breeding, and form yourself upon them. Whatever pleases you most, in others, will infallibly please others, in you. I have often repeated this to you; now is your time of putting it in practice. [*Same date.*]

Little Princes. — In general, I believe that little princes are more likely to be great men than those whose more extensive dominions, and superior strength, flatter them with security; which commonly produces negligence and indolence. A little prince, in the neighborhood of great ones, must be alert, and look out sharp, if he would secure his own dominions; much more still, if he would enlarge them. He must watch for conjunctures, or endeavor to make them. No princes have ever possessed this art better than those of the House of Savoy, who have enlarged their dominions prodigiously within a century, by profiting of conjunctures. [*Same date.*]

Attentions. — A young man should never be wanting in these attentions; they cost little and bring in a great deal, by getting you people's good word and affection. They gain the heart, to which I have always advised you to apply yourself particularly; it guides ten thousand for one that reason influences.

I cannot end this letter, or (I believe) any other, without repeating my recommendation of *the Graces*. They are to be met with at Turin; for God's sake, sacrifice to them, and they will be propitious. People mistake grossly, to imagine that the least awkwardness, in either matter or manner, mind or body, is an indifferent thing, and not worthy of attention. It may possibly be a weakness in me (but in short we are all so made). I confess to you fairly, that when you shall come home, and that I first see you, if I find you ungraceful in your address, and awkward in your person and dress, it will be impossible for me to love you half so well as I should otherwise do, let your intrinsic merit and knowledge be ever so great. [*Same date.*]

English Abroad. — I am informed there are now many English at the Academy at Turin, and I fear those are just so many dangers for you to encounter. Who they are, I do not know; but I well know the general ill conduct, the indecent behavior, and the illiberal views of my young countrymen abroad; especially wherever they are in numbers together. Ill example is of itself dangerous enough; but those who give it seldom stop there; they add their infamous exhortations and invitations; and, if these fail, they have recourse to ridicule, which is harder for one of your age and inexperience to withstand than either of the former. Be upon your guard, therefore, against these batteries, which will all be played upon you. You are not sent abroad to converse with your own countrymen; among them, in general, you will get little knowledge, no languages, and, I am sure, no manners. I desire that you will form no connections, nor (what they impudently call) friendships, with these people; which are, in truth, only combinations and conspiracies against good morals and good manners. [*May 15, 1749.*]

Vices should be Original. — If people had no vices but their own, few would have so many as they have. For my own part, I would sooner wear other people's clothes than their vices; and they would sit upon me just as well. I hope you will have none; but, if ever you have, I beg, at least, they may be all your own. Vices of adoption are, of all others, the most disgraceful and unpardonable. There are degrees in vices, as well as in virtues; and I must do my countrymen the justice to say, they generally take their vices in the lowest degree. Their gallantry is the infamous mean debauchery of stews, justly attended and rewarded by the loss of their health as well as their character. Their pleasures of the table end in beastly drunkenness, low riot, broken windows, and very often (as they well deserve) broken bones. They game for the sake of the vice, not of the amusement; and therefore carry it to excess; undo, or are undone by, their companions. By such conduct, and in such company abroad, they come home the unimproved, illiberal, and ungentlemanlike creatures that one daily sees them; that is, in the park, and in the streets, for one never meets them in good company; where they have neither manners to present themselves, nor merit to be received. But, with the manners of footmen and grooms, they assume their dress too; for you must have observed them in the streets here, in dirty blue frocks, with oaken sticks in their hands, and their hair greasy and unpowdered, tucked up under their hats of an enormous size. Thus finished and adorned by their travels, they become the disturbers of playhouses; they break the windows, and commonly the landlords, of the taverns where they drink; and are at once the support, the terror, and the victims of the bawdy-houses they frequent. These poor mistaken people think they shine, and so they do indeed; but it is as putrefaction shines, in the dark.

I am not now preaching to you, like an old fellow, upon either religious or moral texts; I am persuaded you do not want the best instructions of that kind; but I am advising you as a man, as a friend of the world, as one who would not have you old while you are young, but would have you take all the pleasures that reason points out, and that decency warrants. [*Same date.*]

Foolish Sayings. — There are some expressions, both in French and English, and some characters, both in those two and in other countries, which have, I dare say, misled many young men to their ruin. *Une honnête débauche, une jolie débauche: an agreeable rake, a man of pleasure.* Do not think that this means debauchery and profligacy; nothing like it. It means, at most, the accidental and unfrequent irregularities of youth and vivacity, in opposition to dulness, formality, and want of spirit. [*Same date.*]

How to Please.—You must not neglect your dress neither, but take care to be *bien mis.* Pray send for the best operator for the teeth at Turin, where I suppose there is some famous one, and let him put yours in perfect order; and then take care to keep them so afterwards yourself. You had very good teeth, and I hope they are so still; but even those who have bad ones should keep them clean; for a dirty mouth is, to my mind, ill-manners. In short, neglect nothing that can possibly please. A thousand nameless little things, which nobody can describe but which everybody feels, conspire to form that *whole* of pleasing; as the several pieces of a mosaic work, though separately of little beauty or value, when properly joined form those beautiful figures which please everybody. A look, a gesture, an attitude, a tone of voice, all bear their parts in the great work of pleasing. The art of pleasing is more particularly necessary in your intended profession than perhaps in any other; it is, in truth, the first half of your business; for if you do not please the court you are sent to, you will be of very little use to the court you are sent from. Please the eyes and the ears, they will introduce you to the heart; and, nine times in ten, the heart governs the understanding.

Make your court particularly, and show distinguished attentions, to such men and women as are best at court, highest in the fashion and in the opinion of the public; speak advantageously of them behind their backs, in companies who you have reason to believe will tell them again. Express your admiration of the many great men that the house of Savoy has produced; observe, that nature, instead of being exhausted by those efforts, seems to have redoubled them in the persons of the present king, and the Duke of Savoy; wonder at this rate where it will end, and conclude that it will end in the government of all Europe. Say this, likewise, where it will probably be repeated; but say it unaffectedly, and the last, especially, with a kind of *enjouement.* These little arts are very allowable, and must be made use of in the course of the world; they are pleasing to one party, useful to the other, and injurious to nobody. [*Same date.*]

Flattery.—I recommended to you, in my last, an innocent piece of art; that of flattering people behind their backs, in presence of those who, to make their own court, much more than for your sake, will not fail to repeat, and even amplify the praise to the party concerned. This is of all flattery the most pleasing, and consequently the most effectual. There are other, and many other inoffensive arts of this kind, which are necessary in the course of the world, and which he who practises the earliest, will please the most, and rise the soonest. [*May 22, 1749.*]

Temper. — The principal of these things, is the mastery of one's temper, and that coolness of mind, and serenity of countenance, which hinders us from discovering, by words, actions, or even looks, those passions or sentiments, by which we are inwardly moved or agitated; and the discovery of which, gives cooler and abler people such infinite advantages over us, not only in business, but in all the most common occurrences of life. A man who does not possess himself enough to hear disagreeable things, without visible marks of anger and change of countenance, or agreeable ones without sudden bursts of joy and expansion of countenance, is at the mercy of every artful knave, or pert coxcomb; the former will provoke or please you by design, to catch unguarded words or looks, by which he will easily decipher the secrets of your heart, of which you should keep the key yourself, and trust it with no man living. [*Same date.*]

Immobility. — Determine, too, to keep your countenance as unmoved and unembarrassed as possible which steadiness you may get a habit of, by constant attention. I should desire nothing better, in any negotiation, than to have to do with one of these men of warm, quick passions; which I would take care to set in motion. By artful provocations, I would extort rash and unguarded expressions; and, by hinting at all the several things that I could suspect, infallibly discover the true one, by the alteration it occasioned in the countenance of the person. *Vólto sciolto con pensieri stretti,*40 is a most useful maxim in business. [*Same date.*]

Dissimulation. — It may be objected, that I am now recommending dissimulation to you; I both own and justify it. It has been long said: *Qui nescit dissimulare nescit regnare*: I go still farther, and say, that without some dissimulation, no business can be carried on at all. It is *simulation* that is false, mean and criminal; that is the cunning which Lord Bacon calls crooked or left-handed wisdom, and which is never made use of but by those who have not true wisdom. And the same great man says, that dissimulation is only to hide our own cards; whereas simulation is put on in order to look into other people's. Lord Bolingbroke in his "Idea of a Patriot King," which he has lately published, and which I will send you by the first opportunity, says, very justly, that simulation is a *stiletto*; not only an unjust but an unlawful weapon, and the use of it very rarely to be excused, never justified. Whereas dissimulation is a shield, as secrecy is armor; and it is no more possible to preserve secrecy in business, without some degree of dissimulation, than it is to succeed in business without secrecy. [*Same date.*]

The Face. — Make yourself absolute master, therefore, of your temper, and your countenance, so far, at least, as that no visible change do appear in either, whatever you may feel inwardly. This may be difficult, but it is by no means impossible; and, as a man of sense never attempts impossibilities on one hand, on the other he is never discouraged by difficulties. [*Same date.*]

The Easy Moment.—Some people are to be reasoned, some flattered, some intimidated, and some teased into a thing; but, in general, all are to be brought into it at last, if skilfully applied to, properly managed, and indefatigably attacked in their several weak places. The time should likewise be judiciously chosen: every man has his *mollia tempora*, but that is far from being all day long; and you would choose your time very ill, if you applied to a man about one business, when his head was full of another, or when his heart was full of grief, anger, or any other disagreeable sentiments. [*Same date.*]

Judge of Others by Yourself.—In order to judge of the inside of others, study your own; for men in general are very much alike; and though one has one prevailing passion, and another has another, yet their operations are much the same; and whatever engages or disgusts, pleases or offends you, in others, will, *mutatis mutandis*, engage, disgust, please, or offend others, in you. [*Same date.*]

Smart Sayings.—The temptation of saying a smart and witty thing, or *bon mot*, and the malicious applause with which it is commonly received, have made people who can say them, and, still oftener, people who think they can, but cannot and yet try, more enemies, and implacable ones too, than any one other thing that I know of. When such things, then, shall happen to be said at your expense (as sometimes they certainly will) reflect seriously upon the sentiments of uneasiness, anger, and resentment, which they excite in you; and consider whether it can be prudent, by the same means, to excite the same sentiments in others against you. It is a decided folly to lose a friend for a jest; but, in my mind, it is not a much less degree of folly, to make an enemy of an indifferent and neutral person for the sake of a *bon mot*. When things of this kind happen to be said of you the most prudent way is to seem not to suppose that they are meant at you, but to dissemble and conceal whatever degree of anger you may feel inwardly; and should they be so plain that you cannot be supposed ignorant of their meaning, to join in the laugh of the company against yourself; acknowledge the hit to be a fair one, and the jest a good one, and play off the whole thing in seeming good humor; but by no means reply in the same way; which only shows that you are hurt, and publishes the victory which you might have concealed. Should the thing said, indeed, injure your honor, or moral character, there is but one proper reply; which I hope you will never have occasion to make. [*Same date.*]

Women of Fashion.—They are a numerous and loquacious body; their hatred would be more prejudicial than their friendship can be advantageous to you. A general complaisance and attention to that sex is, therefore, established by custom, and certainly necessary. But where you would particularly please any one, whose situation, interest, or connections can be of use to you, you must show particular preference. The least attentions please, the greatest charm them. The innocent but pleasing flattery of their persons, however gross, is greedily swallowed, and kindly digested, but a seeming regard for their understandings, a seeming desire of, and deference for, their advice, together with a seeming confidence in their moral virtues, turns their head entirely in your favor. Nothing shocks them so much as the least appearance of that contempt, which they are apt to suspect men of entertaining of their capacities; and you may be very sure of gaining their friendship, if you seem to think it worth gaining. Here dissimulation is very often necessary, and even simulation sometimes allowable; which, as it pleases them, may be useful to you and is injurious to nobody. [*Same date.*]

Venetian Art. — The time you will probably pass at Venice will allow you to make yourself master of that intricate and singular form of government, which few of our travellers know anything of. Read, ask, and see everything that is relative to it. There are, likewise, many valuable remains of the remotest antiquity, and many fine pieces of the *antico moderno*, all which deserve a different sort of attention from that which your countrymen commonly give them. They go to see them as they go to see the lions, and kings on horseback, at the Tower here, only to say that they have seen them. You will, I am sure, view them in another light; you will consider them as you would a poem, to which indeed they are akin. You will observe whether the sculptor has animated his stone, or the painter his canvas, into the just expression of those sentiments and passions which should characterize and mark their several figures. [*June 22, 1749.*]

Sculpture and Painting. — You will examine, likewise, whether, in their groups there be a unity of action or proper relation; a truth of dress and manners. Sculpture and painting are very justly called liberal arts; a lively and strong imagination, together with a just observation being absolutely necessary to excel in either, which, in my opinion, is by no means the case of music, though called a liberal art, and now in Italy placed even above the other two — a proof of the decline of that country. A taste of sculpture and painting is, in my mind, as becoming as a taste of fiddling and piping is unbecoming a man of fashion. The former is connected with history and poetry; the latter, with nothing that I know of, but bad company. [*Same date.*]

Amiability. — There is a certain concurrence of various little circumstances, which compose what the French call *l'amiable*; and which, now you are entering into the world, you ought to make it your particular study to acquire. Without them, your learning will be pedantry, your conversation often improper, always unpleasant, and your figure, however good in itself, awkward and unengaging. A diamond while rough has indeed its intrinsic value; but till polished is of no use, and would neither be sought for nor worn. Its great lustre, it is true, proceeds from its solidity and strong cohesion of parts; but without the last polish, it would remain forever a dirty, rough mineral in the cabinets of some few curious collectors. You have, I hope, that solidity and cohesion of parts; take now as much pains to get the lustre. Good company, if you make the right use of it, will cut you into shape, and give you the true brilliant polish. *Apropos* of diamonds, I have sent you, by Sir James Gray, the king's minister, who will be at Venice about the middle of September, my own diamond buckles, which are fitter for your young feet than for my old ones; they will properly adorn you; they would only expose me. [*Same date.*]

Trifles.—Great merit or great failings will make you respected or despised; but trifles, little attentions, mere nothings, either done or neglected, will make you either liked or disliked, in the general run of the world. Examine yourself, why you like such and such people, and dislike such and such others; and you will find that those different sentiments proceed from very slight causes. Moral virtues are the foundation of society in general, and of friendship in particular; but attentions, manners, and graces both adorn and strengthen them. [*July 20, 1749.*]

Youth Armed by Experience.—Your youth and talents, armed with my experience, may go a great way; and that armor is very much at your service, if you please to wear it. I premise that it is not my imagination, but my memory, that gives you these rules; I am not writing pretty, useful reflections. A man of sense soon discovers, because he carefully observes where and how long he is welcome; and takes care to leave the company, at least, as soon as he is wished out of it. Fools never perceive whether they are ill-timed or ill-placed. [*Same date.*]

Idleness.—But indeed I do not suspect you of one single moment's idleness in the whole day. Idleness is only the refuge of weak minds, and the holiday of fools. I do not call good company and liberal pleasures idleness; far from it; I recommend to you a good share of both. [*Same date.*]

Bathing.—I am very glad that my letter, with Dr. Shaw's opinion, has lessened your bathing; for, since I was born, I never heard of bathing four hours a day, which would surely be too much, even in Medea's kettle, if you wanted (as you do not yet) new boiling. [*July 30, 1749.*]

Architecture—A Simile.—To carry on the metaphor of building, I would wish you to be a Corinthian edifice, upon a Tuscan foundation; the latter having the utmost strength and solidity to support, and the former all possible ornaments to decorate. The Tuscan column is coarse, clumsy, and unpleasant; nobody looks at it twice: the Corinthian fluted column is beautiful and attractive; but without a solid foundation, can hardly be seen twice, because it must soon tumble down. Yours affectionately. [*Same date.*]

Earn your Pleasures. — No man tastes pleasures truly who does not earn them by previous business; and few people do business well who do nothing else. Remember, that when I speak of pleasures I always mean the elegant pleasures of a rational being, and not the brutal ones of a swine. I mean *la bonne chere*, short of gluttony; wine, infinitely short of drunkenness; play, without the least gaming; and gallantry, without debauchery. There is a line in all these things which men of sense, for greater security, take care to keep a good deal on the right side of; for sickness, pain, contempt, and infamy lie immediately on the other side of it. Men of sense and merit in all other respects may have had some of these failings; but then those few examples, instead of inviting us to imitation, should only put us the more upon our guard against such weaknesses. Whoever thinks them fashionable will not be so himself. I have often known a fashionable man to have some one vice, but I never, in my life, knew a vicious man a fashionable man. Vice is as degrading as it is criminal. God bless you, my dear child! [*Aug. 7, 1749.*]

Dignity of Manners. — There is a certain dignity of manners absolutely necessary, to make even the most valuable character either respected or respectable. Horse-play, romping, frequent and loud fits of laughter, jokes, waggery, and indiscriminate familiarity, will sink both merit and knowledge into a degree of contempt. They compose at most a merry fellow; and a merry fellow was never yet a respectable man. Indiscriminate familiarity either offends your superiors, or else dubs you their dependent, and led captain. It gives your inferiors just but troublesome and improper claims of equality. A joker is near akin to a buffoon; and neither of them is the least related to wit. Whoever is admitted or sought for in company upon any account than that of his merit and manners, is never respected there, but only made use of. We will have such-a-one, for he sings prettily; we will invite such-a-one to a ball, for he dances well; we will have such-a-one at supper, for he is always joking and laughing; we will ask another, because he plays deep at all games, or because he can drink a great deal. These are vilifying distinctions, mortifying preferences, and exclude all ideas of esteem and regard. Whoever *is had* (as it is called) in company, for the sake of any one thing singly, is singly that thing, and will never be considered in any other light, consequently never respected, let his merits be what they will. [*Aug. 10, 1749.*]

Fools and their Flattery. — Abject flattery and indiscriminate assentation degrade, as much as indiscriminate contradiction and noisy debate disgust.

But a modest assertion of one's own opinion, and a complaisant acquiescence in other people's, preserve dignity.

Vulgar, low expressions, awkward motions and address, vilify, as they imply either a very low turn of mind, or low education, and low company. [*Same date.*]

A Trifler.—Cardinal de Retz, very sagaciously marked out Cardinal Chigi for a little mind, from the moment that he told him he had wrote (*sic*) three years with the same pen, and that it was an excellent good one still.

A certain degree of exterior seriousness, in looks and motions, gives dignity, without excluding wit and decent cheerfulness, which are always serious themselves. A constant smirk upon the face, and a whiffling activity of the body, are strong indications of futility. Whoever is in a hurry shows that the thing he is about is too big for him. Haste and hurry are very different things. [*Same date.*]

The Pretender—Political Caution.—You will, in many parts of Italy, meet with numbers of the Pretender's people (English, Scotch, and Irish fugitives) especially at Rome; and probably the Pretender himself. It is none of your business to declare war on these people; as little as it is your interest, or, I hope, your inclination to connect yourself with them: and therefore I recommend to you a perfect neutrality. Avoid them as much as you can with decency and good manners; but, when you cannot avoid any political conversation or debates with them, tell them that you do not concern yourself with political matters; that you are neither a maker nor a deposer of kings; that, when you left England, you left a king in it, and have not since heard either of his death, or of any revolution that has happened, and that you take kings and kingdoms as you find them; but enter no farther into matters with them, which can be of no use, and might bring on heat and quarrels. When you speak of the old Pretender you will call him only, the Chevalier de St. George; but mention him as seldom as possible. Should he chance to speak to you at any assembly (as, I am told, he sometimes does to the English) be sure that you seem not to know him; and answer him civilly, but always either in French or in Italian; and give him, in the former, the appellation of *Monsieur*, and in the latter of *Signore*. Should you meet with the Cardinal of York, you will be under no difficulty, for he has, as Cardinal, an undoubted right to *Eminenza*. Upon the whole, see any of those people as little as possible; when you do see them be civil to them, upon the footing of strangers; but never be drawn into any altercations with them about the imaginary right of their king, as they call him.

It is to no sort of purpose to talk to those people of the natural rights of mankind and particular constitution of this country. Blinded by prejudices, soured by misfortunes, and tempted by their necessities, they are as incapable of reasoning rightly, as they have hitherto been of acting wisely. The late Lord Pembroke never would know anything that he had not a mind to know; and, in this case, I advise you to follow his example. Never know either the father or the two sons, any otherwise than as foreigners; and so not knowing their pretensions you have no occasion to dispute them. [*Sept. 5, 1749.*]

A Father's Anxiety. — It seems extraordinary, but it is very true, that my anxiety for you increases in proportion to the good accounts which I receive of you from all hands. I promise myself so much from you, that I dread the least disappointment. You are now so near the port, which I have so long wished and labored to bring you safe into, that my concern would be doubled, should you be shipwrecked within sight of it. The object, therefore, of this letter is (laying aside all the authority of the parent), to conjure you as a friend, by the affection you have for me (and surely you have reason to have some), and by the regard you have for yourself, to go on with assiduity and attention, to complete that work, which, of late, you have carried on so well, and which is now so near being finished. My wishes, and my plan, were to make you shine, and distinguish yourself equally in the learned and the polite world. Few have been able to do it. [*Sept. 12, 1749.*]

The Student of Life and the Trifler: A Dialogue. — I will suppose you at Rome, studying six hours uninterruptedly with Mr. Harte, every morning, and passing your evenings with the best company of Rome, observing their manners and forming your own; and I will suppose a number of idle, sauntering, illiterate English, as there commonly is there, living entirely with one another, supping, drinking, and sitting up late at each other's lodgings; commonly in riots and scrapes when drunk, and never in good company when sober. I will take one of these pretty fellows, and give you the dialogue between him and yourself; such as I dare say it will be on his side, and such as I hope it will be on yours.

Englishman. Will you come and breakfast with me to-morrow; there will be four or five of our countrymen; we have provided chaises, and we will drive somewhere out of town after breakfast?

Stanhope. I am very sorry I cannot; but I am obliged to be at home all the morning.

Englishman. Why then we will come and breakfast with you.

Stanhope. I can't do that neither, I am engaged.

Englishman. Well, then, let it be the next day.

Stanhope. To tell you the truth, it can be no day in the morning; for I neither go out, nor see anybody at home before twelve.

Englishman. And what the devil do you do with yourself till twelve o'clock?

Stanhope. I am not by myself, I am with Mr. Harte.

Englishman. Then what the devil do you do with him?

Stanhope. We study different things; we read, we converse.

Englishman. Very pretty amusement indeed! Are you to take orders then?

Stanhope. Yes, my father's orders, I believe, I must take.

Englishman. Why, hast thou no more spirit than to mind an old fellow a thousand miles off?

Stanhope. If I don't mind his orders he won't mind my draughts.

Englishman. What, does the old prig threaten, then? Threatened folks live long; never mind threats.

Stanhope. No, I can't say that he has ever threatened me in his life; but I believe I had best not provoke him.

Englishman. Pooh! you would have one angry letter from the old fellow, and there would be an end of it.

Stanhope. You mistake him mightily; he always does more than he says. He has never been angry with me yet, that I remember, in his life; but if I were to provoke him, I am sure he would never forgive me; he would be coolly immovable, and I might beg and pray, and write my heart out to no purpose.

Englishman. Why then, he is an old dog, that's all I can say: and pray, are you to obey your dry-nurse too, this same what's his name — Mr. Harte?

Stanhope. Yes.

Englishman. So he stuffs you all morning with Greek, and Latin, and logic, and all that. Egad, I have a dry-nurse too, but I never looked into a book with him in my life; I have not so much as seen the face of him this week, and don't care a louse if I never see it again.

Stanhope. My dry-nurse never desires anything of me that is not reasonable, and for my own good; and therefore I like to be with him.

Englishman. Very sententious and edifying, upon my word! at this rate you will be reckoned a very good young man.

Stanhope. Why, that will do me no harm.

Englishman. Will you be with us to-morrow in the evening, then? We shall be ten with you; and I have got some excellent good wine; and we'll be very merry.

Stanhope. I am very much obliged to you but I am engaged for all the evening, to-morrow; first at Cardinal Albani's; and then to sup at the Venetian Embassadress's.

Englishman. How the devil can you like being always with these foreigners? I never go amongst them, with all their formalities and ceremonies. I am never easy in company with them, and I don't know why, but I am ashamed.

Stanhope. I am neither ashamed nor afraid; I am very easy with them; they are very easy with me; I get the language, and I see their characters, by conversing with them; and that is what we are sent abroad for. Is it not?

Englishman. I hate your modest women's company; your women of fashion, as they call 'em. I don't know what to say to them, for my part.

Stanhope. Have you ever conversed with them?

Englishman. No, I never conversed with them; but I have been sometimes in their company, though much against my will.

Stanhope. But at least they have done you no hurt; which is, probably, more than you can say of the women you do converse with.

Englishman. That's true, I own; but for all that, I would rather keep company with my surgeon half the year, than with your women of fashion the year round.

Stanhope. Tastes are different, you know, and every man follows his own.

Englishman. That's true; but thine's a devilish odd one, Stanhope. All morning with thy dry-nurse; all the evening in formal fine company; and all day long afraid of old Daddy in England. Thou art a queer fellow, and I am afraid there's nothing to be made of thee.

Stanhope. I am afraid so, too.

Englishman. Well, then, good-night to you; you have no objection, I hope, to my being drunk to-night, which I certainly will be?

Stanhope. Not in the least; nor to your being sick to-morrow, which you as certainly will be; and so good-night too.

You will observe, that I have not put into your mouth those good arguments, which upon such an occasion would, I am sure, occur to you; as piety and affection towards me; regard and friendship for Mr. Harte; respect for your own moral character, and for all the relative duties of man, son, pupil and citizen. Such solid arguments would be thrown away upon such shallow puppies. Leave them to their ignorance, and to their dirty, disgraceful vices. They will severely feel the effects of them, when it will be too late. Without the comfortable refuge of learning, and with all the sickness and pains of a ruined stomach, and a rotten carcass, if they happen to arrive at old age, it is an uneasy and ignominious one. The ridicule which such fellows endeavor to throw upon those who are not like them is, in the opinion of all men of sense, the most authentic panegyric. Go on, then, my dear child, in the way you are in, only for a year and a half more; that is all I ask of you. After that, I promise that you shall be your own master, and that I will pretend to no other title than that of your best and truest friend. You shall receive advice, but no orders, from me; and in truth you will want no other advice, but such as youth and inexperience must necessarily require. You shall certainly want nothing that is requisite, not only for your conveniency, but also for your pleasures, which I always desire should be gratified. You will suppose that I mean the pleasures *d'un honnête homme*. [*Same date.*]

A Panegyrist.—If I had faith in philters and love potions, I should suspect that you had given Sir Charles Williams some, by the manner in which he speaks of you, not only to me, but to everybody else. I will not repeat to you what he says of the extent and correctness of your knowledge, as it might either make you vain, or persuade you that you had already enough of what nobody can have too much. You will easily imagine how many questions I asked, and how narrowly I sifted him upon your subject; he answered me, and I dare say with truth, just as I could have wished. [*Sept. 22, 1749.*]

Necessity of Attention.—Sir Charles Williams told me then, that in company you were frequently most *provokingly* inattentive, absent, *and distrait*. That you came into a room and presented yourself very awkwardly; that at table you constantly threw down knives, forks, napkins, bread, etc., and that you neglected your person and dress to a degree unpardonable at any age, and much more so at yours.

Distraction and Inattention.—I know no one thing more offensive to a company than that inattention and *distraction*. It is showing them the utmost contempt; and people never forgive contempt. No man is *distrait* with the man he fears or the woman he loves; which is a proof that every man can get the better of that *distraction*, when he thinks it worth his while to do so; and, take my word for it, it is always worth his while. For my own part, I would rather be in company with a dead man than with an absent one; for if the dead man gives me no pleasure, at least he shows me no contempt; whereas the absent man, silently indeed, but very plainly, tells me that he does not think me worth his attention. Besides, can an absent man make any observations upon the characters, customs, and manners of the company? No. He may be in the best companies all his lifetime (if they will admit him, which, if I were they, I would not), and never be one jot the wiser. I never will converse with an absent man; one may as well talk to a deaf one. It is, in truth, a practical blunder to address ourselves to a man who, we see plainly, neither hears, minds, nor understands us. Moreover, I aver that no man is, in any degree, fit for either business or conversation who cannot and does not direct and command his attention to the present object, be that what it will. You know, by experience, that I grudge no expense in your education, but I will positively not keep you a flapper. You may read, in Dr. Swift, the description of these flappers, and the use they were of to their friends.

Dancing. — Learn to dance, not so much for the sake of dancing, as for coming into a room, and presenting yourself genteelly and gracefully. Women, whom you ought to endeavor to please, cannot forgive a vulgar and awkward air and gesture; *il leur faut du brillant*. The generality of men are pretty like them, and are equally taken by the same exterior graces. [*Same date.*]

Finery Unfit for the Old. — I am very glad that you have received the diamond buckles safe: all I desire in return for them is, that they may be buckled upon your feet, and that your stockings may not hide them. I should be sorry you were an egregious fop; but I protest that, of the two, I would rather have you a fop than a sloven. I think negligence in my own dress, even at my age, when certainly I expect no advantages from my dress, would be indecent with regard to others. I have done with fine clothes; but I will have my plain clothes fit me, and made like other people's. In the evenings I recommend to you the company of women of fashion, who have a right to attention, and will be paid it. Their company will smooth your manners, and give you a habit of attention and respect; of which you will find the advantage among men.

My plan for you, from the beginning, has been to make you shine equally in the learned and in the polite world; the former part is almost completed to my wishes, and will, I am persuaded, in a little time more be quite so. The latter part is still in your power to complete; and I flatter myself that you will do it, or else the former part will avail you very little; especially in your department, where the exterior address and graces do half the business; they must be the harbingers of your merit, or your merit will be very coldly received: all can and do judge of the former, few of the latter.

Mr. Harte tells me that you have grown very much since your illness; if you get up to five feet ten, or even nine inches, your figure will, probably, be a good one. [*Same date.*]

Mis-sent Letters. — Our letters go, at best, so irregularly, and so often miscarry totally, that, for greater security, I repeat the same things. So, though I acknowledge by last post Mr. Harte's letter of the 8th September, N. S., I acknowledge it again by this to you.41 [*Same date.*]

Bend to Ceremony. — *Apropos* of the Pope, remember to be presented to him before you leave Rome, and go through the necessary ceremonies for it, whether of kissing his slipper or his breech; for I would never deprive myself of anything that I wanted to do or see by refusing to comply with an established custom. When I was in Catholic countries, I never declined kneeling in their churches at the elevation, nor elsewhere, when the host went by. It is a complaisance due to the custom of the place, and by no means, as some silly people have imagined, an implied approbation of their doctrine. Bodily attitudes and situations are things so very indifferent in themselves, that I would quarrel with nobody about them. It may, indeed, be improper for Mr. Harte to pay that tribute of complaisance, upon account of his character. [*Same date.*]

The Vulgar Man — Trifles — Vulgarism. — A vulgar man is captious and jealous; eager and impetuous about trifles. He suspects himself to be slighted, thinks everything that is said meant at him; if the company happens to laugh, he is persuaded they laugh at him; he grows angry and testy, says something very impertinent, and draws himself into a scrape, by showing what he calls a proper spirit, and asserting himself. A man of fashion does not suppose himself to be either the sole or principal object of the thoughts, looks, or words of the company; and never suspects that he is either slighted or laughed at, unless he is conscious that he deserves it. And if (which very seldom happens) the company is absurd or ill-bred enough to do either, he does not care twopence, unless the insult be so gross and plain as to require satisfaction of another kind. As he is above trifles, he is never vehement and eager about them; and, wherever they are concerned, rather acquiesces than wrangles. A vulgar man's conversation always savors strongly of the lowness of his education and company. It turns chiefly upon his domestic affairs, his servants, the excellent order he keeps in his own family, and the little anecdotes of the neighborhood; all which he relates with emphasis, as interesting matters. He is a man gossip.

Vulgarism in language is the next and distinguishing characteristic of bad company and a bad education. A man of fashion avoids nothing with more care than that. Proverbial expressions, and trite sayings, are the flowers of the rhetoric of a vulgar man. Would he say, that men differ in their tastes, he both supports and adorns that opinion, by the good old saying, as he respectfully calls it, that *what is one man's meat is another man's poison.* If anybody attempts being *smart,* as he calls it, upon him, he gives them *tit for tat,* ay, that he does. He has always some favorite word for the time being, which, for the sake of using often, he commonly abuses.

Such as *vastly* angry, *vastly* kind, *vastly* handsome, and *vastly* ugly. Even his pronunciation of proper words carries the mark of the beast along with it. He calls the earth *yearth*; he is *obleiged* 42 not *obliged* to you. He goes *to wards*, and not towards such a place. He sometimes affects hard words, by way of ornament, which he always mangles like a learned woman. A man of fashion never has recourse to proverbs and vulgar aphorisms: uses neither favorite words nor hard words, but takes great care to speak very correctly and grammatically, and to pronounce properly; that is, according to the usage of the best companies. [*Sept. 27, 1749.*]

Left-handedness. — An awkward address, ungraceful attitudes and actions, and a certain left-handedness (if I may use that word) loudly proclaim low education and low company; for it is impossible to suppose that a man can have frequented good company without having catched something, at least, of their air and motions. A new-raised man is distinguished in a regiment by his awkwardness; but he must be impenetrably dull if, in a month or two's time, he cannot perform at least the common manual exercise, and look like a soldier. The very accoutrements of a man of fashion are grievous incumbrances to a vulgar man. He is at a loss what to do with his hat, when it is not upon his head; his cane (if unfortunately he wears one) is at perpetual war with every cup of tea or coffee he drinks; destroys them first, and then accompanies them in their fall.

A Noble Ease and Grace. — Do not imagine that these accomplishments are only useful with women; they are much more so with men. In a public assembly, what an advantage has a graceful speaker, with genteel motions, a handsome figure, and a liberal air, over one, who shall speak full as much sense, but destitute of these ornaments! In business, how prevalent are the graces, how detrimental is the want of them! By the help of these I have known some men refuse favors less offensively than others granted them. The utility of them in courts and negotiations is inconceivable. You gain the hearts, and consequently the secrets, of nine in ten that you have to do with, in spite even of their prudence; which will, nine times in ten, be the dupe of their hearts and of their senses. Consider the importance of these things as they deserve, and you will not lose one moment in the pursuit of them. [*Same date.*]

The Fribble and the Virtuoso. — No piping nor fiddling, I beseech you; no days lost in poring upon almost imperceptible *intaglios* and *cameos*: and do not become a virtuoso of small wares. Form a taste of painting, sculpture, and architecture, if you please, by a careful examination of the works of the best ancient and modern artists; those are liberal arts, and a real taste and knowledge of them become a man of fashion very well. But, beyond certain bounds, the man of taste ends, and the frivolous virtuoso begins.

Your friend Mendes, the good Samaritan, dined with me yesterday. He has more good nature and generosity, than parts. However, I will show him all the civilities that his kindness to you so justly deserves; he tells me that you are taller than I am, which I am very glad of. I desire you may excel me in everything else too; and, far from repining, I shall rejoice at your superiority. [*Same date.*]

Frequent Letters. — Indeed the irregularity and negligence of the post provoke me, as they break the thread of the accounts I want to receive from you, and of the instructions and orders which I send you almost every post. Of these last twenty posts, I am sure that I have wrote eighteen, either to you or to Mr. Harte, and it does not appear, by your letter, that all, or even any of my letters have been received. I desire, for the future, that both you and Mr. Harte will constantly, in your letters, mention the dates of mine. [*Oct. 2, 1749.*]

Proper Expenses to be Paid. — As to the expense which you mention, I do not regard it in the least; from your infancy to this day, I never grudged any expense in your education, and still less do it now, that it is become more important and decisive. I attend to the objects of your expenses, but not to the sums. I will certainly not pay one shilling for your losing your nose, your money, or your reason; that is, I will not contribute to women, gaming, and drinking. But I will most cheerfully supply, not only every necessary, but every decent expense you can make. I do not care what the best masters cost. I would have you as well dressed, lodged, and attended, as any reasonable man of fashion in his travels. I would have you have that pocket-money that should enable you to make the proper expense, *d'un honnête homme*. In short, I bar no expense, that has neither vice nor folly for its object; and under those two reasonable restrictions, draw and welcome. [*Same date.*]

A Portrait. — So many of my letters have miscarried, and I know so little which, that I am forced to repeat the same thing over and over again eventually. This is one. I have wrote twice to Mr. Harte, to have your picture drawn in miniature, while you were at Venice, and to send it me in a letter: it is all one to me, whether in enamel or in water-colors, provided it is but very like you. I would have you drawn exactly as you are, and in no whimsical dress. I lay more stress upon the likeness of the picture, than upon the taste and skill of the painter. If this be not already done, I desire that you will have it done forthwith, before you leave Venice; and enclose it in a letter to me; which letter, for greater security, I would have you desire Sir James Gray to enclose in his packet to the office; as I, for the same reason, send this under his cover. If the picture be done upon vellum, it will be the most portable. Send me, at the same time, a thread or silk of your own length, exactly. I am solicitous about your figure; convinced, by a thousand instances, that a good one is a real advantage. *Mens sana in corpore sano,* is the first and greatest blessing. I would add, *et pulchro,* to complete it. May you have that, and every other! Adieu. [*Same date.*]

A Century Ago. — The papal power, founded originally upon the ignorance and superstition of mankind, extended by the weakness of some princes, and the ambition of others; is declining of late, in proportion as knowledge has increased; and owing its present precarious security not to the religion, the affection, or the fear, of the temporal powers, but to their jealousy of each other. The Pope's excommunications are no longer dreaded; his indulgences little solicited, and sell very cheap; and his territories, formidable to no power, are coveted by many, and will, most undoubtedly, within a century, be scantled out among the great powers, who have now a footing in Italy; whenever they can agree upon the division of the bear's skin. [*Oct. 9, 1749.*]

The Jesuits. — They have, by turns, been banished, and with infamy, almost every country in Europe; and have always found means to be restored, even with triumph. In short, I know no government in the world that is carried on upon such deep principles of policy, I will not add morality. Converse with them, frequent them, court them; *but know them.*

Inform yourself too of that infernal court, the inquisition; which, though not so considerable at Rome as in Spain and Portugal, will, however, be a good sample to you of what the villainy of some men can contrive, the folly of others receive, and both together establish; in spite of the first natural principles of reason, justice, and equity. [*Same date.*]

Military Study. — Go with some engineer or old officer, and view, with care, the real fortifications of some strong place; and you will get a clearer idea of bastions, half-moons, horn-works, ravelins, glacis, etc., than all the masters in the world could give you upon paper. And thus much I would, by all means, have you know of both civil and military architecture. [*Oct. 17, 1749.*]

A Father's Object. — Dear Boy: From the time that you have had life, it has been the principal and favorite object of mine, to make you as perfect as the imperfections of human nature will allow; in this view I have grudged no pains nor expense in your education; convinced that education, more than nature, is the cause of that great difference which we see in the characters of men. While you, were a child, I endeavored to form your heart habitually to virtue and honor, before your understanding was capable of showing you their beauty and utility. Those principles, which you then got like your grammar rules, only by rote, are now, I am persuaded, fixed and confirmed by reason. And indeed they are so plain and clear, that they require but a very moderate degree of understanding, either to comprehend or practice them. Lord Shaftesbury says, very prettily, that he would be virtuous for his own sake, though nobody were to know it; as he would be clean for his own sake, though nobody were to see him. I have therefore, since you have had the use of your reason, never written to you upon those subjects; they speak best for themselves; and I should, now, just as soon think of warning you gravely not to fall into the dirt or the fire, as into dishonor or vice. [*Nov. 5, 1749.*]

Good Breeding.— A friend of yours and mine has very justly defined good breeding to be *the result of much good sense, some good nature, and a little self-denial for the sake of others, and with a view to obtain the same indulgence from them*. Taking this for granted (as I think it cannot be disputed), it is astonishing to me, that anybody, who has good sense and good nature (and I believe you have both), can essentially fail in good breeding. As to the modes of it, indeed, they vary according to persons, places, and circumstances; and are only to be acquired by observation and experience; but the substance of it is everywhere and eternally the same. Good-manners are, to particular societies, what good morals are to society in general—their cement and their security. And as laws are enacted to enforce good morals, or at least to prevent the ill-effects of bad ones, so there are certain rules of civility, universally implied and received, to enforce good manners, and punish bad ones. And indeed there seems to be less difference, both between the crimes and punishments, than at first one would imagine. The immoral man, who invades another's property, is justly hanged for it; and the ill-bred man, who, by his ill-manners, invades and disturbs the quiet comforts of private life, is by common consent as justly banished from society. Mutual complaisances, attentions, and sacrifices of little conveniences, are as natural an implied compact between civilized people, as protection and obedience are between kings and subjects; whoever, in either case, violates that compact, justly forfeits all advantages arising from it. For my own part, I really think that, next to the consciousness of doing a good action, that of doing a civil one is the most pleasing; and the epithet which I should covet the most, next to that of Aristides, would be that of well-bred. [*Same date.*]

Mixed   Company—Learning—Pedants.—In   mixed   companies, whoever is admitted to make part of them is, for the time at least, supposed to be upon a footing of equality with the rest; and, consequently, as there is no one principal object of awe and respect, people are apt to take a greater latitude in their behavior, and to be less upon their guard; and so they may, provided it be within certain bounds, which are upon no occasion to be transgressed. But, upon these occasions, though no one is entitled to distinguished marks of respect, every one claims, and very justly, every mark of civility and good breeding. Ease is allowed, but carelessness and negligence are strictly forbidden. If a man accosts you, and talks to you ever so dully or frivolously, it is worse than rudeness, it is brutality, to show him, by a manifest inattention to what he says, that you think him a fool or a blockhead, and not worth hearing. It is much more so with regard to women; who, of whatever rank they are, are entitled, in consideration of their sex, not only to an attentive, but an officious good breeding from men.

Not too much Familiarity. — The most familiar and intimate habitudes, connections, and friendships require a degree of good breeding both to preserve and cement them. If ever a man and his wife, or a man and his mistress, who pass nights as well as days together, absolutely lay aside all good breeding, their intimacy will soon degenerate into a coarse familiarity, infallibly productive of contempt or disgust. The best of us have our bad sides; and it is as imprudent, as it is ill-bred, to exhibit them. I shall certainly not use ceremony with you; it would be misplaced between us: but I shall certainly observe that degree of good breeding with you, which is, in the first place, decent, and which, I am sure, is absolutely necessary to make us like one another's company long.

The deepest learning, without good breeding, is unwelcome and tiresome pedantry, and of use nowhere but in a man's own closet; and consequently of little or no use at all.

A man, who is not perfectly well-bred, is unfit for good company, and unwelcome in it; will consequently dislike it soon, afterward renounce it; and be reduced to solitude, or, what is worse, low and bad company.

A man, who is not well-bred, is full as unfit for business as for company.

Make then, my dear child, I conjure you, good breeding the great object of your thoughts and actions at least half the day. Observe carefully the behavior and manners of those who are distinguished by their good breeding; imitate, nay, endeavor to excel, that you may at least reach them; and be convinced that good breeding is, to all worldly qualifications, what charity is to all Christian virtues. Observe how it adorns merit, and how often it covers the want of it. May you wear it to adorn, and not to cover you! Adieu. [*Same date.*]

Personal Graces. — These personal graces are of very great consequence. They anticipate the sentiments, before merit can engage the understanding; they captivate the heart, and gave rise, I believe, to the extravagant notions of charms and philters. Their efforts were so surprising, that they were reckoned supernatural. The most graceful and best-bred men, and the handsomest and genteelest women, give the most philters; and, as I verily believe, without the least assistance of the Devil. Pray be not only well dressed, but shining in your dress; let it have *du brillant*: I do not mean by a clumsy load of gold and silver, but by the taste and fashion of it. Women like and require it; they think it an attention due to them. [*Nov. 14, 1749.*]

Dancing Youth.—You danced pretty well here, and ought to dance very well before you come home; for what one is obliged to do sometimes, one ought to be able to do well. Besides, *la belle danse donne du brillant à un jeune homme.* And you should endeavor to shine. A calm serenity, negative merit and graces, do not become your age. You should be *alerte, adroit, vif;* be wanted, talked of, impatiently expected, and unwillingly parted with in company. I should be glad to hear half a dozen women of fashion say: "*Où est donc le petit Stanhope? Que ne vient-il? Il faut avouer qu'il est aimable.*" All this I do not mean singly with regard to women as the principal object; but with regard to men, and with a view of your making yourself considerable. For, with very small variations, the same things that please women please men. [*Same date.*]

Ill Breeding.—My last was upon the subject of good breeding; but, I think, it rather set before you the unfitness and disadvantages of ill breeding, than the utility and necessity of good; it was rather negative than positive. This, therefore, shall go further, and explain to you the necessity, which you, of all people living, lie under, not only of being positively and actively well-bred, but of shining and distinguishing yourself by your good breeding. Consider your own situation in every particular, and judge whether it is not essentially your interest, by your own good breeding to others, to secure theirs to you; and that, let me assure you, is the only way of doing it; for people will repay, and with interest too, inattention with inattention, neglect with neglect, and ill-manners with worse; which may engage you in very disagreeable affairs. In the next place your profession requires, more than any other, the nicest and most distinguished good breeding. You will negotiate with very little success, if you do not, previously, by your manners, conciliate and engage the affections of those with whom you are to negotiate. Can you ever get into the confidence and the secrets of the courts where you may happen to reside, if you have not those pleasing, insinuating manners, which alone can procure them? Upon my word, I do not say too much, when I say that superior good breeding, insinuating manners, and genteel address are half your business. Your knowledge will have but very little influence upon the mind, if your manners prejudice the heart against you; but, on the other hand, how easily will you *dupe* the understanding, where you have first engaged the heart? and hearts are, by no means, to be gained by that mere common civility which everybody practises. Bowing again to those who bow to you, answering dryly those who speak to you, and saying nothing offensive to anybody, is such negative good breeding that it is only not being a brute; as it would be but a very poor commendation of any man's cleanliness to say that he did not stink. It is an active, cheerful, officious, seducing good breeding that must gain you the good-will and first sentiments of the men, and the affections of the women. You must carefully watch and attend to their passions, their tastes, their little humors and weaknesses, and *aller au devant.* You must do it, at the same time, with alacrity and *empressement,* and not as if you graciously condescended to humor their weaknesses.

For instance; suppose you invited anybody to dine or sup with you, you ought to recollect if you had observed that they had any favorite dish, and take care to provide it for them: and, when it came, you should say: *"You seemed to me, at such and such a place, to give this dish a preference, and therefore I ordered it. This is the wine that I observed you liked, and therefore I procured some."* The more trifling these things are, the more they prove your attention for the person, and are consequently the more engaging. Consult your own breast, and recollect how these little attentions, when shown you by others, flatter that degree of self-love and vanity, from which no man living, is free. Reflect how they incline and attract you to that person, and how you are propitiated afterward to all which that person says or does. The same causes will have the same effects in your favor.

Attentions to Ladies. — Women, in a great degree, establish or destroy every man's reputation of good breeding; you must, therefore, in a manner, overwhelm them with the attentions of which I have spoken; they are used to them, they expect them; and, to do them justice, they commonly requite them. You must be sedulous, and rather over officious than under, in procuring them their coaches, their chairs, their conveniences in public places; not see what you should not see; and rather assist, where you cannot help seeing. Opportunities of showing these attentions present themselves perpetually; but if they do not, make them. As Ovid advises his lover, when he sits in the *circus* near his mistress, to wipe the dust off her neck, even if there be none. *Si nullus, tamen excute nullum.* Your conversation with women should always be respectful; but, at the same time, *enjoué,* and always addressed to their vanity. Everything you say or do should convince them of the regard you have (whether you have it or not) for their beauty, their wit, or their merit. Men have possibly as much vanity as women, though of another kind; and both art and good breeding require that, instead of mortifying, you should please and flatter it, by words and looks of approbation. Suppose (which is by no means improbable) that, at your return to England, I should place you near the person of some one of the royal family; in that situation, good breeding, engaging address, adorned with all the graces that dwell at courts, would very probably make you a favorite, and from a favorite, a minister; but all the knowledge and learning in the world, without them, never would. The penetration of princes seldom goes deeper than the surface. It is the exterior that always engages their hearts; and I would never advise you to give yourself much trouble about their understandings. Princes in general (I mean those *Porphyrogenets* who are born and bred in purple) are about the pitch of women; bred up like them, and are to be addressed and gained in the same manner. They always see, they seldom weigh. Your lustre, not your solidity, must take them; your inside will afterward support and secure what your outside has acquired. With weak people (and they undoubtedly are three parts in four of mankind) good breeding, address, and manners are everything; they can go no deeper; but let me assure you that they are a great deal, even with people of the best understandings. Where the eyes are not pleased, the heart is not flattered, the mind will be apt to stand out. Be this right or wrong, I confess I am so made myself. Awkwardness and ill breeding shock me, to that degree, that where I meet with them, I cannot find in my heart to inquire into the intrinsic merit of that person; I hastily decide in myself that he can have none; and am not sure I should not even be sorry to know that he had any. I often paint you in my imagination, in your present *lontananza*; and, while I view you in the light of ancient and modern learning, useful and ornamental knowledge, I am charmed with the prospect; but when I view you in another light, and represent you awkward, ungraceful, ill-bred, with vulgar air and manners, shambling towards me with inattention and *distractions*, I shall not pretend to describe to you what I feel; but will do as a skilful painter did formerly, draw a veil before the countenance of the father.

I dare say you know already enough of architecture, to know that the Tuscan is the strongest and most solid of all the orders; but, at the same time, it is the coarsest and clumsiest of them. Its solidity does extremely well for the foundation and base floor of a great edifice; but, if the whole building be Tuscan, it will attract no eyes, it will stop no passengers, it will invite no interior examination; people will take it for granted that the finishing and furnishing cannot be worth seeing, where the front is so unadorned and clumsy. But if, upon the solid Tuscan foundation, the Doric, the Ionic, and the Corinthian orders, rise gradually with all their beauty, proportions, and ornaments, the fabric seizes the most incurious eye, and stops the most careless passenger; who solicits admission as a favor, nay, often purchases it. Just so will it fare with your little fabric, which, at present, I fear, has more of the Tuscan than the Corinthian order. You must absolutely change the whole front, or nobody will knock at the door. The several parts, which must compose this new front, are elegant, easy, natural, superior good breeding; an engaging address; genteel motions; an insinuating softness in your looks, words, and actions; a spruce, lively air, and fashionable dress; and all the glitter that a young fellow should have. [*No date.*]

Learning and Politeness. — I have often asserted, that the profoundest learning, and the politest manners, were by no means incompatible, though so seldom found united in the same person; and I have engaged myself to exhibit you, as a proof of the truth of this assertion. Should you, instead of that, happen to disprove me, the concern indeed will be mine, but the loss will be yours. Lord Bolingbroke is a strong instance on my side of the question; he joins, to the deepest erudition, the most elegant politeness and good breeding that ever any courtier and man of the world was adorned with. And Pope very justly called him All Accomplished St. John, with regard to his knowledge and his manners. He had, it is true, his faults; which proceeded from unbounded ambition and impetuous passions; but they have now subsided by age and experience; and I can wish you nothing better than to be, what he is now, without being what he has been formerly. His address pre-engages, his eloquence persuades, and his knowledge informs all who approach him. Upon the whole, I do desire, and insist, that, from after dinner till you go to bed, you make good breeding, address, and manners your serious object and your only care. Without them, you will be nobody; with them, you may be anything. [*No date.*]

Proper Distinction. — Every rational being (I take it for granted) proposes to himself some object more important than mere respiration and obscure animal existence. He desires to distinguish himself among his fellow-creatures; and *alicui negotio intentus, præclari facinoris, aut artis bonæ, famam quærit.* Cæsar, when embarking, in a storm, said, that it was not necessary he should live; but that it was absolutely necessary he should get to the place to which he was going. And Pliny leaves mankind this only alternative; either of doing what deserves to be written, or of writing what deserves to be read. As for those who do neither, *eorum vitam mortemque juxta æstumo; quoniam de utraque siletur.* You have, I am convinced, one or both of these objects in view; but you must know, and use the necessary means, or your pursuit will be vain and frivolous. In either case, *capere est principium et fons*; but it is by no means all. That knowledge must be adorned, it must have lustre as well as weight, or it will be oftener taken for lead than for gold. Knowledge you have, and will have; I am easy upon that article. But my business, as your friend, is not to compliment you upon what you have, but to tell you with freedom what you want; and I must tell you plainly, that I fear you want everything but knowledge. [*Nov. 24, 1749.*]

Style.—It is not every understanding that can judge of matter; but every ear can and does judge, more or less, of style; and were I either to speak or write to the public, I should prefer moderate matter, adorned with all the beauties and elegancies of style, to the strongest matter in the world, ill worded and ill delivered. Your business is, negotiation abroad, and oratory in the House of Commons at home. What figure can you make in either case, if your style be inelegant, I do not say bad? Imagine yourself writing an office-letter to a secretary of state, which letter is to be read by the whole cabinet council, and very possibly afterward, laid before parliament; any one barbarism, solecism, or vulgarism in it would, in a very few days, circulate through the whole kingdom, to your disgrace and ridicule. For instance; I will suppose you had written the following letter from The Hague to the secretary of state at London, and leave you to suppose the consequences of it:

"My Lord,—I *had*, last night, the honor of your lordship's letter, of the 24th; and will *set about doing* the orders contained *therein*; and *if so be* that I can get that affair done by the next post, I will not fail *for to* give your lordship an account of it by *next post*. I have told the French minister *as how*, *that if* that affair be not soon concluded, your lordship would think it *all long of him*; and that he must have neglected *for to* have wrote to his court about it. I must beg leave to put your lordship in mind, *as how*, that I am now full three quarters in arrear; and if *so be* that I do not very soon receive at least one half year, I shall *cut a very bad figure*; for *this here* place is very dear. I shall be *vastly beholden* to your lordship for *that there* mark of your favor; and so I *rest*, or *remain*, Yours," etc.

You will tell me, possibly, that this is a *caricatura* of an illiberal and inelegant style; I will admit it; but assure you, at the same time, that a dispatch with less than half these faults would blow you up forever. It is by no means sufficient to be free from faults in speaking and writing; you must do both correctly and elegantly. [*Same date.*]

Mispronunciation and Misuse of Words.—A person of the House of Commons, speaking two years ago upon naval affairs, asserted, that we had then the finest navy *upon the face of the yearth*. This happy mixture of blunder and vulgarism, you may easily imagine, was matter of immediate ridicule; but I can assure you that it continues so still, and will be remembered as long as he lives and speaks. Another, speaking in defence of a gentleman, upon whom a censure was moved, happily said that he thought that gentleman was more *liable* to be thanked and rewarded, than censured. You know, I presume, that *liable* can never be used in a good sense. [*Same date.*]

Books for Oratory.—You have read Quintilian—the best book in the world to form an orator; pray read *Cicero, de Oratore*—the best book in the world to finish one. Translate and retranslate, from and to Latin, Greek, and English; make yourself a pure and elegant English style: it requires nothing but application. I do not find that God has made you a poet; and I am very glad that he has not; therefore, for God's sake, make yourself an orator, which you may do. Though I still call you a boy, I consider you no longer as such; and when I reflect upon the prodigious quantity of manure that has been laid upon you, I expect you should produce more at eighteen, than uncultivated soils do at eight and twenty. [*Same date.*]

Chesterfield a Censor-Critic. — While the Roman republic flourished, while glory was pursued and virtue practised, and while even little irregularities and indecencies, not cognizable by law, were, however, not thought below the public care, censors were established, discretionally to supply, in particular cases, the inevitable defects of the law, which must, and can only be general. This employment I assume to myself, with regard to your little republic, leaving the legislative power entirely to Mr. Harte; I hope, and believe, that he will seldom, or rather never, have occasion to exert his supreme authority; and I do by no means suspect you of any faults that may require that interposition. But, to tell you the plain truth, I am of opinion, that my censorial power will not be useless to you, nor a *sinecure* to me. The sooner you make it both, the better for us both. I can now exercise this employment only upon hearsay, or, at most, written evidence; and therefore shall exercise it with great lenity, and some diffidence; but when we meet, and that I can form my judgment upon ocular and auricular evidence, I shall no more let the least impropriety, indecorum, or irregularity pass uncensured, than my predecessor Cato did. I shall read you with the attention of a critic, not with the partiality of an author: different in this respect, indeed, from most critics, that I shall seek for faults only to correct, and not to expose them. [*Nov. 26, 1749.*]

Nicknames. — The little defects in manners, elocution, address, and air (and even of figure, though very unjustly), are the objects of ridicule, and the causes of nicknames. You cannot imagine the grief it would give me, and the prejudice it would do you, if, by way of distinguishing you from others of your name, you should happen to be called Muttering Stanhope, Absent Stanhope, Ill-bred Stanhope, or Awkward, Left-legged Stanhope; therefore, take great care to put it out of the power of ridicule itself to give you any of these ridiculous epithets; for, if you get one, it will stick to you like the envenomed shirt. The very first day that I see you, I shall be able to tell you, and certainly shall tell you, what degree of danger you are in; and I hope that my admonitions, as censor, may prevent the censures of the public. [*Same date.*]

Young Stanhope's Portrait. — I send you here a portrait, drawn by a lady at Venice, by my orders: "In compliance to your orders, I have examined young Stanhope carefully, and think I have penetrated into his character. This is his portrait, which I take to be a faithful one. His face is pleasing, his countenance sensible, and his look clever. His figure is at present rather too square; but if he shoots up, which he has matter and years for, he will then be of a good size. He has, undoubtedly, a great fund of acquired knowledge; I am assured that he is master of the learned languages. As for French, I know he speaks it perfectly, and I am told German, as well. The questions he asks are judicious, and denote a thirst after knowledge. I cannot say that he appears equally desirous of pleasing, for he seems to neglect attentions and the graces. He does not come into a room well, nor has he that easy, noble carriage, which would be proper for him. It is true, he is as yet young and inexperienced; one may therefore reasonably hope that his exercises, which he has not yet gone through, and good company, in which he is still a novice, will polish, and give all that is wanting to complete him. What seems necessary for that purpose, would be an attachment to some woman of fashion, and who knows the world. Some Madame de L'Ursay would be the proper person. In short, I can assure you that he has everything which Lord Chesterfield can wish him, excepting that carriage, those graces, and the style used in the best company; which he will certainly acquire in time, and by frequenting the polite world. If he should not, it would be great pity, since he so well deserves to possess them. You know their importance. My lord, his father, knows it too, he being master of them all. To conclude, if little Stanhope acquires the graces, I promise you he will make his way; if not, he will be stopped in a course, the goal of which he might attain with honor."43

Man Unrational, yet all Men the same in Feeling. — Those who suppose that men in general act rationally, because they are called rational creatures, know very little of the world; and if they act themselves upon that supposition, will, nine times in ten, find themselves grossly mistaken. That man is, *animal bipes, implume, risibile*, I entirely agree; but for the *rationale*, I can only allow it him in *actu primo* (to talk logic), and seldom *in actu secundo*. Thus, the speculative, cloistered pedant, in his solitary cell, forms systems of things, as they should be, not as they are; and writes as decisively and absurdly upon war, politics, manners, and characters, as that pedant talked, who was so kind as to instruct Hannibal in the art of war. Such closet politicians never fail to assign the deepest motives for the most trifling actions; instead of often ascribing the greatest actions to the most trifling causes, in which they would be much seldomer mistaken. They read and write of kings, heroes, and statesmen, as never do anything but upon the deepest principles of sound policy. But those who see and observe kings, heroes, and statesmen, discover that they have headaches, indigestions, humors, and passions, just like other people; every one of which, in their turns, determine their wills, in defiance of their reason. [*Dec. 5, 1749.*]

Charm of Manner. — The late Lord Townshend always spoke materially, with argument and knowledge, but never pleased. Why? His diction was not only inelegant, but frequently ungrammatical, always vulgar; his cadences false, his voice unharmonious, and his action ungraceful. Nobody heard him with patience; and the young fellows used to joke upon him, and repeat his inaccuracies. The late Duke of Argyle, though the weakest reasoner, was the most pleasing speaker I ever knew in my life. He charmed, he warmed, he forcibly ravished the audience; not by his matter certainly, but by his manner of delivering it. A most genteel figure, a graceful, noble air, an harmonious voice, an elegancy of style, and a strength of emphasis, conspired to make him the most affecting, persuasive, and applauded speaker I ever saw. I was captivated like others; but when I came home, and coolly considered what he had said, stripped of all those ornaments in which he had dressed it, I often found the matter flimsy, the arguments weak, and I was convinced of the power of those adventitious concurring circumstances, which ignorance of mankind only, calls trifling ones. [*Same date.*]

Tickling Follies. — If you will please people, you must please them in their own way; and, as you cannot make them what they should be, you must take them as they are. I repeat it again, they are only to be taken by *agrémens*, and by what flatters their senses and their hearts. Rabelais first wrote a most excellent book, which nobody liked; then, determined to conform to the public taste, he wrote "Gargantua and Pantagruel," which everybody liked, extravagant as it was. Adieu. [*Same date.*]

True Elocution. — What then does all this mighty heart and mystery of speaking in Parliament amount to? Why, no more than this, that the man who speaks in the House of Commons, speaks in that house, and to four hundred people, that opinion, upon a given subject, which he would make no difficulty of speaking in any house in England, round the fire, or at table, to any fourteen people whatsoever; better judges, perhaps, and severer critics of what he says, than any fourteen gentlemen of the House of Commons.

I have spoken frequently in Parliament, and not always without some applause; and therefore I can assure you, from my experience, that there is very little in it. The elegancy of the style, and the turn of the periods, make the chief impression upon the hearers. Give them but one or two round and harmonious periods in a speech, which they will retain and repeat, and they will go home as well satisfied, as people do from an opera, humming all the way one or two favorite tunes that have struck their ears and were easily caught. Most people have ears, but few have judgment; tickle those ears, and, depend upon it, you will catch their judgments, such as they are. [*Dec. 9, 1749.*]

Hampden a Lesson. — Lord Clarendon, in his history, says of Mr. John Hampden, *that he had a head to contrive, a tongue to persuade, and a hand to execute, any mischief.* I shall not now enter into the justness of this character of Mr. Hampden, to whose brave stand against the illegal demand of ship-money, we owe our present liberties; but I mention it to you as the character, which, with the alteration of one single word, *good,* instead of *mischief,* I would have you aspire to, and use your utmost endeavors to deserve. The head to contrive, God must to a certain degree have given you; but it is in your own power greatly to improve it, by study, observation, and reflection. As for the *tongue to persuade,* it wholly depends upon yourself; and without it the best head will contrive to very little purpose. The hand to execute depends, likewise, in my opinion, in a great measure upon yourself. Serious reflection will always give courage in a good cause; and the courage arising from reflection is of a much superior nature to the animal and constitutional courage of a foot-soldier. The former is steady and unshaken, where the *nodus* is *dignus vindice;* the latter is oftener improperly than properly exerted, but always brutally. [*Dec. 12, 1749.*]

Things of Consequence — Bolingbroke. — He thought all these things of consequence, and he thought right; pray do you think so too? It is of the utmost consequence to you to be of that opinion. If you have the least defect in your elocution, take the utmost care and pains to correct it. Do not neglect your style, whatever language you speak in, or whomever you speak to, were it your footman. Seek always for the best words and the happiest expressions you can find. Do not content yourself with being barely understood; but adorn your thoughts, and dress them as you would your person; which, however well proportioned it might be, it would be very improper and indecent to exhibit naked, or even worse dressed than people of your sort are.

I have sent you, in a packet which your Leipsic acquaintance, Duval, sends to his correspondent at Rome, Lord Bolingbroke's book,[44] which he published about a year ago. I desire that you will read it over and over again, with particular attention to the style, and to all those beauties of oratory with which it is adorned. Till I read that book, I confess I did not know all the extent and powers of the English language. Lord Bolingbroke has both a tongue and a pen to persuade. [*Same date.*]

Complicated Machines. — I have often told you (and it is most true) that, with regard to mankind, we must not draw general conclusions from certain particular principles, though, in the main, true ones. We must not suppose that, because a man is a rational animal, he will, therefore, always act rationally; or, because he has such or such a predominant passion, that he will act invariably and consequentially in the pursuit of it. No, we are complicated machines; and though we have one main spring that gives motion to the whole, we have an infinity of little wheels, which, in their turns, retard, precipitate, and sometimes stop that motion. [*Dec. 19, 1749.*]

Ambition and Avarice. — There are two inconsistent passions, which, however, frequently accompany each other, like man and wife; and which, like man and wife too, are commonly clogs upon each other. I mean ambition and avarice: the latter is often the true cause of the former; and then is the predominant passion. It seems to have been so in Cardinal Mazarin; who did anything, submitted to anything, and forgave anything, for the sake of plunder. He loved and courted power like a usurer; because it carried profit along with it. Whoever should have formed his opinion, or taken his measures, singly, from the ambitious part of Cardinal Mazarin's character, would have found himself often mistaken. Some, who had found this out, made their fortunes by letting him cheat them at play. On the contrary, Cardinal Richelieu's prevailing passion seems to have been ambition, and his immense riches, only the natural consequences of that ambition gratified; and yet, I make no doubt but that ambition had now and then its turn with the former, and avarice with the latter. Richelieu (by the way) is so strong a proof of the inconsistency of human nature, that I cannot help observing to you that, while he absolutely governed both his king and his country, and was, in a great degree, the arbiter of the fate of all Europe, he was more jealous of the great reputation of Corneille, than of the power of Spain; and more flattered with being thought (what he was not) the best poet, than with being thought (what he certainly was) the greatest statesman in Europe; and affairs stood still, while he was concerting the criticism upon the *Cid.* Could one think this possible, if one did not know it to be true? [*Same date.*]

Women, Vanity, and Love. — Women are much more like each other than men; they have, in truth, but two passions, vanity and love: these are their universal characteristics. An Agrippina may sacrifice them to ambition, or a Messalina to lust; but such instances are rare; and, in general, all they say, and all they do, tends to the gratification of their vanity, or their love. He who flatters them most pleases them best; and they are most in love with him who they think is the most in love with them. No adulation is too strong for them; no assiduity too great; no simulation of passion too gross; as, on the other hand, the least word or action, that can possibly be construed into a slight or contempt, is unpardonable, and never forgotten. Men are, in this respect, tender, too, and will sooner forgive an injury than an insult. Some men are more captious than others; some are always wrongheaded; but every man living has such a share of vanity, as to be hurt by marks of slight and contempt. Every man does not pretend to be a poet, a mathematician, or a statesman, and considered as such; but every man pretends to common-sense, and to fill his place in the world with common decency; and, consequently, does not easily forgive those negligencies, inattentions, and slights, which seem to call in question, or utterly deny him, both these pretensions. [*Same date.*]

Too Ready Friends.—Be upon your guard against those who, upon very slight acquaintance, obtrude their unasked and unmerited friendship and confidence upon you; for they probably cram you with them only for their own eating; but, at the same time, do not roughly reject them upon that general supposition. Examine further, and see whether those unexpected offers flow from a warm heart and a silly head, or a designing head and a cold heart; for knavery and folly have often the same symptoms. In the first case, there is no danger in accepting them, *valeant quantum valere possunt.* In the latter case, it may be useful to seem to accept them, and artfully to turn the battery upon him who raised it.

There is an incontinency of friendship among young fellows, who are associated by their mutual pleasures only; which has, very frequently, bad consequences. A parcel of warm hearts, and unexperienced heads, heated by convivial mirth, and possibly a little too much wine, vow, and really mean at the time, eternal friendships to each other, and indiscreetly pour out their whole souls in common, and without the least reserve. These confidences are as indiscreetly repealed, as they were made; for new pleasures, and new places, soon dissolve this ill cemented connection; and then very ill uses are made of these rash confidences. Bear your part, however, in young companies; nay, excel, if you can, in all the social and convivial joy and festivity that become youth. Trust them with your love tales, if you please; but keep your serious views secret. [*Same date.*]

The Gentler Virtues.—Cæsar had all the great vices, and Cato all the great virtues, that men could have. But Cæsar had the *leniores virtutes*, which Cato wanted; and which made him beloved, even by his enemies, and gained him the hearts of mankind, in spite of their reason; while Cato was not even beloved by his friends, notwithstanding the esteem and respect which they could not refuse to his virtues; and I am apt to think that if Cæsar had wanted, and Cato possessed, those *leniores virtutes*, the former would not have attempted (at least with success), and the latter could have protected, the liberties of Rome. Mr. Addison, in his Cato, says of Cæsar (and I believe with truth):

"Curse on his virtues, they've undone his country."

Pride and Pedantry.—The costive liberality of a purse-proud man insults the distresses it sometimes relieves; he takes care to make you feel your own misfortunes, and the difference between your situation and his; both which he insinuates to be justly merited: yours, by your folly; his, by his wisdom. The arrogant pedant does not communicate, but promulgates his knowledge. He does not give it to you, but he inflicts it upon you; and is (if possible) more desirous to show you your own ignorance, than his own learning. Such manners as these, not only in the particular instances which I have mentioned, but likewise in all others, shock and revolt that little pride and vanity, which every man has in his heart; and obliterate in us the obligation for the favor conferred, by reminding us of the motive which produced and the manner which accompanied it. [*No date.*]

Greetings and Good Wishes.—The New Year is the season in which custom seems more particularly to authorize civil and harmless lies, under the name of compliments. People reciprocally profess wishes, which they seldom form; and concern, which they seldom feel. That is not the case between you and me, where truth leaves no room for compliments.

Dii tibi dent annos, de te nam cætera sumes, was said formerly to one, by a man who certainly did not think it. With the variation of one word only, I will with great truth say it to you. I will make the first part conditional, by changing, in the second, the *nam* into *si.* May you live, as long as you are fit to live, but no longer! or, may you rather die, before you cease to be fit to live, than after! My true tenderness for you makes me think more of the manner than of the length of your life, and forbids me to wish it prolonged, by a single day, that should bring guilt, reproach, and shame upon you. I have not malice enough in my nature to wish that to my greatest enemy. You are the principal object of all my cares, the only object of all my hopes: I have now reason to believe, that you will reward the former, and answer the latter; in that case, may you live long, for you must live happy; *de te nam cætera sumes.* Conscious virtue is the only solid foundation of all happiness; for riches, power, rank, or whatever, in the common acceptation of the word, is supposed to constitute happiness, will never quiet, much less cure, the inward pangs of guilt. To that main wish I will add those of the good old nurse of Horace, in his Epistle to Tibullus: *Sapere,* you have it in a good degree already. *Et fari ut possit quæ sentiat.* Have you that? More, much more, is meant by it, than common speech, or mere articulation. I fear that still remains to be wished for, and I earnestly wish it you. *Gratia* and *fama* will inevitably accompany the above-mentioned qualifications. The *valetudo* is the only one that is not in your own power, Heaven alone can grant it you, and may it do so abundantly! As for the *mundus victus, non deficiente crumenâ,* do you deserve, and I will provide them. [*Dec. 26, 1749.*]

Poets and Orators. — A man who is not born with a poetical genius can never be a poet, or, at best, an extreme bad one: but every man, who can speak at all, can speak elegantly and correctly, if he pleases, by attending to the best authors and orators; and, indeed, I would advise those who do not speak elegantly, not to speak at all; for, I am sure, they will get more by their silence than by their speech. As for politeness; whoever keeps good company, and is not polite, must have formed a resolution, and taken some pains not to be so; otherwise he would naturally and insensibly acquire the air, the address, and the tone of those he converses with. [*Same date.*]

Method of Study — the World and Books. — Your first morning hours, I would have you devote to your graver studies with Mr. Harte; the middle part of the day, I would have employed in seeing things; and the evenings, in seeing people. You are not, I hope, of a lazy, inactive turn, in either body or mind; and, in that case, the day is full long enough for everything; especially at Rome, where it is not the fashion, as it is here and at Paris, to embezzle at least half of it at table. But if, by accident, two or three hours are sometimes wanting for some useful purpose, borrow them from your sleep. Six, or at most seven hours' sleep is, for a constancy, as much as you or anybody can want: more is only laziness and dozing; and is, I am persuaded, both unwholesome and stupefying. If, by chance, your business, or your pleasures, should keep you up till four or five o'clock in the morning, I would advise you, however, to rise exactly at your usual time, that you may not lose the precious morning hours; and that the want of sleep may force you to go to bed earlier the next night. This is what I was advised to do when very young, by a very wise man; and what, I assure you, I always did in the most dissipated part of my life. I have very often gone to bed at six in the morning, and rose, notwithstanding, at eight; by which means I got many hours, in the morning, that my companions lost; and the want of sleep obliged me to keep good hours the next, or at least the third night. To this method I owe the greatest part of my reading; for, from twenty to forty, I should certainly have read very little, if I had not been up while my acquaintances were in bed. Know the true value of time; snatch, seize, and enjoy every moment of it. No idleness, no laziness, no procrastination: never put off till to-morrow what you can do to-day. That was the rule of the famous and unfortunate pensionary De Witt; who, by strictly following it, found time, not only to do the whole business of the republic, but to pass his evenings at assemblies and suppers, as if he had nothing else to do or think of. [*Same date.*]

Religion, why Silent on. — I have seldom or never written to you upon the subject of religion and morality: your own reason, I am persuaded, has given you true notions of both; they speak best for themselves; but, if they wanted assistance, you have Mr. Harte at hand, both for precept and example: to your own reason, therefore, and to Mr. Harte, shall I refer you, for the reality of both; and confine myself, in this letter, to the decency, the utility, and the necessity of scrupulously preserving the appearances of both. When I say the appearances of religion, I do not mean that you should act or talk like a missionary, or an enthusiast, nor that you should take up a controversial cudgel against whoever attacks the sect you are of; this would be both useless and unbecoming your age; but I mean that you should by no means seem to approve, encourage, or applaud those libertine notions, which strike at religions equally, and which are the poor, threadbare topics of half wits and minute philosophers. Even those who are silly enough to laugh at their jokes are still wise enough to distrust and detest their characters; for, putting moral virtues at the highest, and religion at the lowest, religion must still be allowed to be a collateral security, at least, to virtue; and every prudent man will sooner trust to two securities than to one. Whenever, therefore, you happen to be in company with those pretended *esprits forts*, or with thoughtless libertines, who laugh at all religion, to show their wit, or disclaim it, to complete their riot, let no word or look of yours indicate the least approbation; on the contrary, let a silent gravity express your dislike: but enter not into the subject, and decline such unprofitable and indecent controversies. Depend upon this truth, that every man is the worse looked upon, and the less trusted, for being thought to have no religion; in, spite of all the pompous and specious epithets he may assume of *esprit fort* free-thinker, or moral philosopher; and a wise atheist (if such a thing there is) would, for his own interest and character in this world, pretend to some religion. [*Jan. 8, 1750.*]

Moral Character.—Your moral character must be not only pure, but, like Cæsar's wife, unsuspected. The least speck or blemish upon it is fatal. Nothing degrades and vilifies more, for it excites and unites detestation and contempt. There are, however, wretches in the world profligate enough to explode all notions of moral good and evil; to maintain that they are merely local, and depend entirely upon the customs and fashions of different countries: nay, there are still, if possible, more unaccountable wretches; I mean, those who affect to preach and propagate such absurd and infamous notions, without believing them themselves. These are the Devil's hypocrites. Avoid, as much as possible, the company of such people; who reflect a degree of discredit and infamy upon all who converse with them. But as you may, sometimes, by accident, fall into such company, take great care that no complaisance, no good humor, no warmth of festal mirth, ever make you seem even to acquiesce, much less to approve or applaud, such infamous doctrines. On the other hand, do not debate, nor enter into serious argument, upon a subject so much below it: but content yourself with telling these *apostles*, that you know they are not serious, that you have a much better opinion of them than they would have you have, and that you are very sure they would not practise the doctrine they preach. But put your private mark upon them, and shun them for ever afterwards. [*Same date.*]

Value of Character. — Show yourself, upon all occasions, the advocate, the friend, but not the bully, of virtue. Colonel Chartres,45 whom you have certainly heard of (who was, I believe, the most notorious blasted rascal in the world, and who had, by all sorts of crimes, amassed immense wealth), was so sensible of the disadvantage of a bad character that I heard him once say, in his impudent, profligate manner, that though he would not give one farthing for virtue, he would give ten thousand pounds for a character, because he should get a hundred thousand pounds by it; whereas he was so blasted that he had no longer an opportunity of cheating people. Is it possible, then, that an honest man can neglect what a wise rogue would purchase so dear? [*Same date.*]

A Nice Distinction — Exaggeration. — Lord Bacon, very justly, makes a distinction between simulation and dissimulation, and allows the latter rather than the former; but still observes that they are the weaker sort of politicians who have recourse to either. A man who has strength of mind and strength of parts wants neither of them. "Certainly," says he, "the ablest men that ever were have all had an openness and frankness of dealing, and a name of certainty and veracity; but then they were like horses well managed, for they could tell, passing well, when to stop or turn; and at such times, when they thought the case indeed required some dissimulation, if then they used it, it came to pass that the former opinion spread abroad, of their good faith and clearness of dealing, made them almost invisible." There are people who indulge themselves in a sort of lying, which they reckon innocent, and which in one sense is so; for it hurts nobody but themselves. This sort of lying is the spurious offspring of vanity, begotten upon folly. These people deal in the marvellous; they have seen some things that never existed: they have seen other things which they never really saw, though they did exist, only because they were thought worth seeing. Has anything remarkable been said or done in any place, or in any company? they immediately present and declare themselves eye or ear witnesses of it. They have done feats themselves, unattempted, or at least unperformed by others. They are always the heroes of their own fables, and think that they gain consideration, or at least present attention, by it. Whereas, in truth, all they get is ridicule and contempt, not without a good degree of distrust: for one must naturally conclude that he who will tell any lie from idle vanity will not scruple telling a greater for interest. [*Same date.*]

The Novice in Society. — I remember that when, with all the awkwardness and rust of Cambridge about me, I was first introduced into good company, I was frightened out of my wits. I was determined to be what I thought civil; I made fine low bows, and placed myself below everybody; but when I was spoken to, or attempted to speak myself, *obstupui, steteruntque comæ et vox faucibus hæsit*. If I saw people whisper, I was sure it was at me; and I thought myself the sole object of either the ridicule or the censure of the whole company, who, God knows, did not trouble their heads about me. In this way I suffered, for some time, like a criminal at the bar; and should certainly have renounced all polite company forever, if I had not been so convinced of the absolute necessity of forming my manners upon those of the best companies, that I determined to persevere, and suffer anything, or everything, rather than not compass that point. Insensibly it grew easier to me; and I began not to bow so ridiculously low, and to answer questions without great hesitation or stammering; if, now and then, some charitable people, seeing my embarrassment, and being *désœuvré* themselves, came and spoke to me, I considered them as angels sent to comfort me; and that gave me a little courage. I got more soon afterward, and was intrepid enough to go up to a fine woman, and tell her that I thought it a warm day; she answered me, very civilly, that she thought so too; upon which the conversation ceased, on my part, for some time, till she, good-naturedly resuming it, spoke to me thus: "I see your embarrassment, and I am sure that the few words you said to me cost you a great deal; but do not be discouraged for that reason, and avoid good company. We see that you desire to please, and that is the main point; you want only the manner, and you think that you want it still more than you do. You must go through your noviciate before you can profess good breeding; and, if you will be my novice, I will present you to my acquaintance as such." [*Jan. 11, 1750.*]

The Chaperone. — There is a sort of veteran women (*sic*) of condition, who, having lived always in the *grand monde*, and having possibly had some gallantries, together with the experience of five and twenty or thirty years, form a young fellow better than all the rules that can be given him. These women, being past their bloom, are extremely flattered by the least attention from a young fellow; and they will point out to him those manners and *attentions* that pleased and engaged them, when they were in the pride of their youth and beauty. Wherever you go, make some of those women your friends, which a very little matter will do. Ask their advice, tell them your doubts or difficulties as to your behavior; but take great care not to drop one word of their experience; for experience implies age, and the suspicion of age, no woman, let her be ever so old, ever forgives. [*Same date.*]

Necessary Accomplishments.—I here subjoin a list of all those necessary, ornamental accomplishments (without which no man living can either please or rise in the world), which hitherto I fear you want, and which only require your care and attention to possess.

To speak elegantly whatever language you speak in; without which nobody will hear you with pleasure, and, consequently, you will speak to very little purpose.

An agreeable and distinct elocution; without which nobody will hear you with patience; this everybody may acquire who is not born with some imperfection in the organs of speech. You are not; and therefore it is wholly in your power. You need take much less pains for it than Demosthenes did.

A distinguished politeness of manners and address; which common-sense, observation, good company, and imitation will infallibly give you, if you will accept of it.

A genteel carriage, and graceful motions, with the air of a man of fashion. A good dancing master, with some care on your part, and some imitation of those who excel, will soon bring this about.

To be extremely clean in your person, and perfectly well dressed, according to the fashion, be that what it will. Your negligence of dress, while you were a schoolboy, was pardonable, but would not be so now.

Upon the whole, take it for granted, that, without these accomplishments, all you know, and all you can do, will avail you very little. Adieu. [*Jan. 18, 1750.*]

Time—its Value.—Very few people are good economists of their fortune, and still fewer of their time; and yet, of the two, the latter is the most precious. I heartily wish you to be a good economist of both; and you are now of an age to begin to think seriously of these two important articles. Young people are apt to think they have so much time before them, that they may squander what they please of it, and yet have enough left; as very great fortunes have frequently seduced people to a ruinous profusion. Fatal mistakes, always repented of, but always too late! Old Mr. Lowndes, the famous Secretary of the Treasury, in the reigns of King William, Queen Anne, and King George the First, used to say, "*Take care of the pence, and the pounds will take care of themselves.*" To this maxim, which he not only preached, but practised, his two grandsons, at this time, owe the very considerable fortunes that he left them. [*Feb. 5, 1750.*]

Lazy People—Dispatch—How to Read.—Many people lose a great deal of their time by laziness; they loll and yawn in a great chair, tell themselves that they have not time to begin anything then, and that it will do as well another time. This is a most unfortunate disposition, and the greatest obstruction to both knowledge and business. At your age, you have no right nor claim to laziness; I have, if I please, being *emeritus*. You are but just listed in the world, and must be active, diligent, indefatigable. If ever you propose commanding with dignity, you must serve up to it with diligence. Never put off till to-morrow what you can do to-day.

Dispatch is the soul of business; and nothing contributes more to dispatch than method. Lay down a method for everything, and stick to it inviolably, as far as unexpected incidents may allow. Fix one certain hour and day in the week for your accompts, and keep them together in their proper order; by which means they will require very little time, and you can never be much cheated. Whatever letters and papers you keep, docket and tie them up in their respective classes, so that you may instantly have recourse to any one. Lay down a method also for your reading, for which you allot a certain share of your mornings; let it be in a consistent and consecutive course, and not in that desultory and immethodical manner, in which many people read scraps of different authors, upon different subjects. Keep a useful and short commonplace book of what you read, to help your memory only, and not for pedantic quotations. Never read history without having maps, and a chronological book, or tables, lying by you, and constantly recurred to; without which history is only a confused heap of facts. One method more I recommend to you, by which I have found great benefit, even in the most dissipated part of my life; that is, to rise early, and at the same hour every morning, how late soever you may have sat up the night before. This secures you an hour or two, at least, of reading and reflection, before the common interruptions of the morning begin; and it will save your constitution, by forcing you to go to bed early, at least one night in three. [*Feb. 5, 1750.*]

Dignity in Pleasure. — There is a certain dignity to be kept up in pleasures, as well as in business. In love, a man may lose his heart with dignity; but if he loses his nose, he loses his character into the bargain. At table, a man may with decency have a distinguishing palate; but indiscriminate voraciousness degrades him to a glutton. A man may play with decency; but if he games, he is disgraced. Vivacity and wit make a man shine in company; but trite jokes and loud laughter reduce him to a buffoon. Every virtue, they say, has its kindred vice; every pleasure, I am sure, has its neighboring disgrace. Mark carefully, therefore, the line that separates them, and carefully stop a yard short, than step an inch beyond it.

I wish to God that you had as much pleasure in following my advice, as I have in giving it you; and you may the easier have it, as I give you none that is inconsistent with your pleasure. [*Same date.*]

False Wit. — To do justice to the best English and French authors; they have not given in to that false taste; they allow no thoughts to be good, that are not just, and founded upon truth. The age of Louis XIV. was very like the Augustan; Boileau, Molière, La Fontaine, Racine, etc., established the true, and exposed the false taste. The reign of King Charles II. (meritorious in no other respect) banished false tastes out of England, and proscribed puns, quibbles, acrostics, etc. Since that, false wit has renewed its attacks, and endeavored to recover its lost empire, both in England and France, but without success; though, I must say, with more success in France than in England: Addison, Pope and Swift, having vigorously defended the rights of good-sense, which is more than can be said of their contemporary French authors, who have of late had a great tendency to *le faux brillant, le ranfiement, et l'entortillement*. And Lord Roscommon would be more in the right now, than he was then, in saying, that

"The English bullion of one sterling line,

Drawn to French wire, would through whole pages shine."

[*Same date.*]

No Stoic. — I confess, the pleasures of high life are not always strictly philosophical; and I believe a stoic would blame my indulgence; but I am yet no stoic, though turned of five-and-fifty; and I am apt to think that you are rather less so, at eighteen. The pleasures of the table, among people of the first fashion, may, indeed, sometimes, by accident, run into excesses; but they will never sink into a continued course of gluttony and drunkenness. The gallantry of high life, though not strictly justifiable, carries, at least, no external marks of infamy about it. [*March 8, 1750.*]

Etiquette. — I did not think that the present Pope46 was a sort of man to build seven modern little chapels at the expense of so respectable a piece of antiquity as the *Coliseum*. However, let his holiness' taste of *vertu* be ever so bad, pray get somebody to present you to him, before you leave Rome; and without hesitation kiss his slipper, or whatever else the *etiquette* of that court requires. I would have you see all those ceremonies; and I presume that you are, by this time, ready enough at Italian to understand and answer *il Santo Padre* in that language. [*March 19, 1750.*]

Bibliomania. — When you return here, I am apt to think that you will find something better to do than to run to Mr. Osborne's at Gray's-Inn, to pick up scarce books. Buy good books, and read them; the best books are the commonest, and the last editions are always the best, if the editors are not blockheads; for they may profit of the former. But take care not to understand editions and title-pages too well. It always smells of pedantry, and not always of learning. What curious books I have, they are indeed but few, shall be at your service. I have some of the Old Collana, and the Macchiavel of 1550. Beware of the *Bibliomanie*. [*Same date.*]

Constitutional Monarchy. — England is now the only monarchy in the world that can properly be said to have a constitution; for the people's rights and liberties are secured by laws. I cannot reckon Sweden and Poland to be monarchies. [*March 29, 1750.*]

Aim High. — Aim at perfection in everything, though in most things it is unattainable; however, they who aim at it, and persevere, will come much nearer it than those whose laziness and despondency, make them give it up as unattainable. *Magnis tamen excidit ausis* is a degree of praise which will always attend a noble and shining temerity, and a much better sign in a young fellow, than *serpere humi, tutus nimium timidusque procellæ*, for men, as well as women. [*May 24, 1750.*]

A Due Return. — I heard with great satisfaction the other day, from one who has been lately at Rome, that nobody was better received in the best companies than yourself. The same thing, I dare say, will happen to you at Paris, where they are particularly kind to all strangers who will be civil to them and show a desire of pleasing. But they must be flattered a little, not only by words, but by a seeming preference given to their country, their manners, and their customs; which is but a small price to pay for a very good reception. Were I in Africa, I would pay it to a negro for his good-will. Adieu. [*June 5, 1750.*]

Use of Oratory. — Your trade is to speak well, both in public and in private. The manner of your speaking is full as important as the matter, as more people have ears to be tickled than understandings to judge. Be your productions ever so good, they will be of no use if you stifle and strangle them in their birth. The best compositions of Corelli, if ill executed, and played out of tune, instead of touching, as they do when well performed, would only excite the indignation of the hearers, when murdered by an unskilful performer. But to murder your own productions, and that *coram populo*, is a *Medean cruelty*, which Horace absolutely forbids. Remember of what importance Demosthenes, and one of the Gracchi, thought *enunciation*; read what stress Cicero and Quintilian lay upon it; even the herb-women at Athens were correct judges of it. Oratory with all its graces, that of enunciation in particular, is full as necessary in our government, as it ever was in Greece or Rome. No man can make a fortune or a figure in this country, without speaking, and speaking well in public. [*July 9, 1750.*]

Speak Well. — Recite pieces of eloquence, declaim scenes of tragedies to Mr. Harte, as if he were a numerous audience. If there is any particular consonant which you have a difficulty in articulating, as I think you had with the *R*, utter it millions and millions of times, till you have uttered it right. Never speak quick, till you have first learned to speak well. In short, lay aside every book and every thought, that does not directly tend to this great object, absolutely decisive of your future fortune and figure. [*Same date.*]

A Truth. — Pleasure is necessarily reciprocal; no one feels who does not at the same time give it. To be pleased, one must please. What pleases you in others, will in general please them in you. [*Same date.*]

Learned Ignorance. — A man of the best parts, and the greatest learning, if he does not know the world by his own experience and observation, will be very absurd, and consequently very unwelcome in company. He may say very good things; but they will probably be so ill-timed, misplaced, or improperly addressed, that he had much better hold his tongue. Full of his own matter, and uninformed of, or inattentive to, the particular circumstances and situations of the company, he vents it indiscriminately; he puts some people out of countenance; he shocks others; and frightens all, who dread what may come out next. The most general rule that I can give you for the world, and which your experience will convince you of the truth of, is: Never to give the tone to the company, but to take it from them; and to labor more to put them in conceit with themselves, than to make them admire you. Those whom you can make like themselves better, will, I promise you, like you very well. [*Aug. 6, 1750.*]

A Portrait. — It is Lady Hervey,47 whom I directed you to call upon at Dijon; but who, to my great joy, because to your great advantage, passes all this winter at Paris. She has been bred all her life at courts; of which she has acquired all the easy good breeding and politeness, without the frivolousness. She has all the reading that a woman should have: and more than any woman need have; for she understands Latin perfectly well, though she wisely conceals it. As she will look upon you as her son, I desire that you will look upon her as my delegate: trust, consult, and apply to her without reserve. No woman ever had, more than she has, *le ton de la parfaitement bonne compagnie, les manières engageantes et le je ne sais quoi qui plaît.* Desire her to reprove and correct any, and every, the least error and inaccuracy in your manners, air, addresses, etc. No woman in Europe can do it so well; none will do it more willingly, or in a more proper and obliging manner. [*Oct. 22, 1750.*]

History. — While you are in France, I could wish that the hours you allot for historical amusement should be entirely devoted to the history of France. One always reads history to most advantage in that country to which it is relative, not only books but persons being ever at hand to solve the doubts and clear up difficulties. I do by no means advise you to throw away your time in ransacking, like a dull antiquarian, the minute and important parts of remote and fabulous times. Let blockheads read what blockheads wrote. A general notion of the history of France, from the conquest of that country by the Franks, to the reign of Lewis the Eleventh, is sufficient for use, consequently sufficient for you. There are, however, in those remote times, some remarkable eras, that deserve more particular attention; I mean those in which some notable alterations happened in the constitution and form of government. [*Nov. 1, 1750.*]

Small Talk. — I am far from meaning by this, that you should always be talking wisely, in company, of books, history, and matters of knowledge. There are many companies which you will and ought to keep, where such conversations would be misplaced and ill-timed; your own good sense must distinguish the company, and the time. You must trifle with triflers, and be serious only with the serious, but dance to those who pipe. *Cur in theatrum Cato severe venisti?* was justly said to an old man; how much more so would it be to one of your age? From the moment that you are dressed, and go out, pocket all your knowledge with your watch, and never pull it out in company unless desired: the producing of the one unasked implies that you are weary of the company; and the producing of the other unrequired will make the company weary of you. Company is a republic too jealous of its liberties to suffer a dictator even for a quarter of an hour; and yet in that, as in all republics, there are some who really govern, but then it is by seeming to disclaim, instead of attempting to usurp, the power; that is the occasion in which manners, dexterity, address, and the undefinable *je ne sais quoi* triumph; if properly exerted, their conquest is sure, and the more lasting for not being perceived. Remember, that this is not only your first and greatest, but ought to be almost your only object, while you are in France. [*Same date.*]

A Rake. — Having mentioned the word rake, I must say a word or two more upon that subject, because young people too frequently, and always fatally, are apt to mistake that character for that of a man of pleasure; whereas, there are not in the world two characters more different. A rake is a composition of all the lowest, most ignoble, degrading, and shameful vices; they all conspire to disgrace his character, and to ruin his fortune; while wine and disease contend which shall soonest and most effectually destroy his constitution. A dissolute, flagitious footman, or porter, makes full as good a rake as a man of the first quality. By the by, let me tell you, that in the wildest part of my youth I never was a rake, but, on the contrary, always detested and despised the character.48 [*Nov. 8, 1750.*]

Keep the Peace. — Keep carefully out of all scrapes and quarrels. They lower a character extremely; and are particularly dangerous in France;

where a man is dishonored by not resenting an affront, and utterly ruined by resenting it. The young Frenchmen are hasty, giddy, and petulant; extremely national, and *avantageux*. Forbear from any national jokes or reflections, which are always improper, and commonly unjust. The colder northern nations generally look upon France as a whistling, singing, dancing, frivolous nation; this notion is very far from being a true one, though many *petits maîtres* by their behavior seem to justify it; but those very *petits maîtres*, when mellowed by age and experience, very often turn out very able men. The number of great generals and statesmen, as well as excellent authors, that France has produced, is an undeniable proof, that it is not that frivolous, unthinking, empty nation that the northern prejudices suppose it. [*No date.*]

A New Constitution.—This epigram in Martial:

"Non amo te, Sabidi, nec possum dicere quare,

Hoc tantum possum dicere, non amo te"—49

has puzzled a great many people; who cannot conceive how it is possible not to love anybody, and yet not to know the reason why. I think I conceive Martial's meaning very clearly, though the nature of epigram, which is to be short, would not allow him to explain it more fully; and I take it to be this: "O Sabidis, you are a very worthy, deserving man; you have a thousand good qualities, you have a great deal of learning; I esteem, I respect, but for the soul of me, I cannot love you, though I cannot particularly say why. You are not amiable; you have not those engaging manners, those pleasing attentions, those graces, and that address, which are absolutely necessary to please, though impossible to define. I cannot say it is this or that particular thing which hinders me from loving you, it is the whole together; and upon the whole you are not agreeable." How often have I, in the course of my life, found myself in this situation, with regard to many of my acquaintance, whom I have honored and respected, without being able to love? I did not know why, because, when one is young, one does not take the trouble, nor allow one's self the time, to analyze one's sentiments, and to trace them up to their source. [*Feb. 28, 1751.*]

Carriage of the Body.—It sounds ridiculously to bid you study with your dancing master; and yet I do. The bodily carriage and graces are of infinite consequence to everybody, and more particularly to you. Adieu for this time, my dear child. Yours tenderly. [*No date.*]

How to Please.—An air, a tone of voice, a composure of countenance to mildness and softness, which are all easily acquired, do the business;

and without further examination, and possibly with the contrary qualities, that man is reckoned the gentlest, the modestest, and the best-natured man alive. Happy the man who, with a certain fund of parts and knowledge, gets acquainted with the world early enough to make it his bubble, at an age when most people are the bubbles of the world! for that is the common case of youth. They grow wiser when it is too late; and, ashamed and vexed at having been bubbles so long, too often turn knaves at last. Do not, therefore, trust to appearances and outside yourself, but pay other people with them, because you may be sure that nine in ten of mankind do, and ever will, trust to them. This is by no means a criminal or blamable simulation, if not used with an ill intention. I am by no means blamable in desiring to have other people's good word, good-will, and affection, if I do not mean to abuse them. Your heart, I know, is good, your sense is sound, and your knowledge extensive. [*May 6, 1751.*]

Pictures. — I received yesterday, at the same time, your letters of the 4th and the 11th, N. S., and being much more careful of my commissions than you are of yours, I do not delay one moment sending you my final instructions concerning the pictures. The man, you allow to be a Titian, and in good preservation; the woman is an indifferent and a damaged picture; but, as I want them for furniture for a particular room, companions are necessary; and therefore I am willing to take the woman, for better for worse, upon account of the man; and if she is not too much damaged, I can have her tolerably repaired, as many a fine woman is, by a skilful hand here; but then I expect the lady should be, in a manner, thrown into the bargain with the man; and in this state of affairs, the woman being worth little or nothing, I will not go above fourscore louis for the two together. As for the Rembrandt you mention, though it is very cheap, if good, I do not care for it. I love *la belle nature*; Rembrandt paints caricatures. Now for your own commissions, which you seem to have forgotten. [*May 10, 1751.*]

Dancing and Deportment. — Lady Hervey, who is your puff and panegyrist, writes me word, that she saw you lately dance at a ball, and that you dance very genteelly. I am extremely glad to hear it; for (by the maxim that *omne majus continet in se minus*) if you dance genteelly, I presume you walk, sit, and stand genteelly too; things which are much more easy, though much more necessary, than dancing well. I have known many very genteel people, who could not dance well; but I never knew anybody dance very well, who was not genteel in other things. You will probably often have occasion to stand in circles, at the levees of princes and ministers, when it is very necessary, *de payer de sa personne, et d'être bien planté*, with your feet not too near nor too distant from each other. More people stand and walk, than sit genteelly. Awkward, ill-bred people, being ashamed, commonly sit up bolt upright and stiff; others, too negligent and easy, *se vautrent dans leur fauteuil*, which is ungraceful and ill-bred, unless where the familiarity is extreme. [*June 10, 1751.*]

Little Nothings.—I know a man, and so do you, who, without a grain of merit, knowledge, or talents, has raised himself millions of degrees above his level, simply by a good air and engaging manners; insomuch that the very prince, who raised him so high, calls him, *mon aimable vaurien* 50 : but of this do not open your lips, *pour cause.* I give you this secret, as the strongest proof imaginable, of the efficacy of air, address, *tournure, et tous ces petits riens.* [*Same date.*]

Ease of Manner.—*Les bienséances* 51 are a most necessary part of the knowledge of the world. They consist in the relations of persons, things, time, and place; good sense points them out, good company perfects them (supposing always an attention and a desire to please), and good policy recommends them.

Were you to converse with a king, you ought to be as easy and unembarrassed as with your own valet de chambre; but yet every look, word, and action should imply the utmost respect. What would be proper and well-bred with others much your superiors, would be absurd and ill-bred with one so very much so. You must wait till you are spoken to; you must receive, not give, the subject of conversation, and you must even take care that the given subject of such conversation do not lead you into any impropriety. [*June 13, 1751.*]

Social Respect.—In mixed companies with your equals (for in mixed companies all people are to a certain degree equal) greater ease and liberty are allowed; but they too have their bounds within *bienséance.* There is a social respect necessary; you may start your own subject of conversation with modesty, taking great care, however, *de ne jamais parler de cordes dans la maison d'un pendu.* Your words, gestures, and attitudes have a greater degree of latitude, though by no means an unbounded one. You may have your hands in your pockets, take snuff, sit, stand, or occasionally walk, as you like; but I believe you would not think it very *bienséant* to whistle, put on your hat, loosen your garters or your buckles, lie down upon a couch, or go to bed, and welter in an easy chair. These are negligences and freedoms which one can only take when quite alone; they are injurious to superiors, shocking and offensive to equals, brutal and insulting to inferiors. That easiness of carriage and behavior, which is exceedingly engaging, widely differs from negligence and inattention, and by no means implies that one may do whatever one pleases. [*Same date.*]

Respect due to Woman.—To women you should always address yourself with great outward respect and attention, whatever you feel inwardly; their sex is by long prescription entitled to it; and it is among the duties of *bienséance*; at the same time that respect is very properly, and very agreeably, mixed with a degree of *enjouement*, if you have it; but then, that *badinage* must either directly or indirectly tend to their praise, and even not be liable to a malicious construction to their disadvantage. But here, too, great attention must be had to the difference of age, rank, and situation. A *maréchale* of fifty must not be played with like a young coquette of fifteen; respect and *serious enjouement*, if I may couple those two words, must be used with the former, and mere *badinage, zesté même d'un peu de polissonerie*, is pardonable with the latter. [*Same date.*]

Horse-Laughter.—Loud laughter is extremely inconsistent with *les bienséances*, as it is only the illiberal and noisy testimony of the joy of the mob, at some very silly thing. A gentleman is often seen, but very seldom heard, to laugh. Nothing is more contrary to *les bienséances* than horse-play, or *jeux de main* of any kind whatever, and has often very serious, sometimes very fatal consequences. Romping, struggling, throwing things at one another's head, are the becoming pleasantries of the mob, but degrade a gentleman; *giuoco di mano, giuoco di villano*, is a very true saying, among the few true sayings of the Italians.

There is a *bienséance* also with regard to people of the lowest degree; a gentleman observes it with his footman, even with the beggar in the street. He considers them as objects of compassion, not of insult; he speaks to neither *d'un ton brusque*, but corrects the one coolly, and refuses the other with humanity. There is no one occasion in the world in which *le ton brusque* is becoming a gentleman. In short, *les bienséances* are another word for *manners*. [*Same date.*]

The Two Ages.—Now that all tumultuous passions and quick sensations have subsided with me, and that I have no tormenting cares nor boisterous pleasures to agitate me, my greatest joy is to consider the fair prospect you have before you, and to hope and believe you will enjoy it. You are already in the world, at an age when others have hardly heard of it. Your character is hitherto not only unblemished in its moral part, but even unsullied by any low, dirty, and ungentlemanlike vice; and will, I hope, continue so. Your knowledge is sound, extensive, and avowed, especially in everything relative to your destination. With such materials to begin, what then is wanting? Not fortune, as you have found by experience. You have had, and shall have, fortune sufficient to assist your merit and your industry; and, if I can help it, you never shall have enough to make you negligent of either. You have, too, *mens sana in corpore sano*, the greatest blessing of all. All, therefore, that you want is as much in your power to acquire, as to eat your breakfast when set before you; it is only that knowledge of the world, that elegancy of manners, that universal politeness, and those graces, which keeping good company, and seeing variety of places and characters, must inevitably, with the least attention on your part, give you. Your foreign destination leads to the greatest things, and your parliamentary situation will facilitate your progress; consider then this pleasing prospect as attentively for yourself, as I consider it for you. Labor on your part to realize it, as I will on mine to assist and enable you to do it. *Nullum numen abest, si sit prudentia. [Same date.]*

A Reference at Court. — I would wish you to be able to talk upon all these things, better and with more knowledge than other people; insomuch that, upon those occasions, you should be applied to, and that people should say, *I dare say Mr. Stanhope can tell us.* Second-rate knowledge, and middling talents, carry a man farther at courts, and in the busy part of the world, than superior knowledge and shining parts. Tacitus very justly accounts for a man's having always kept in favor, and enjoyed the best employments, under the tyrannical reigns of three or four of the very worst emperors, by saying that it was not *propter aliquam eximiam artem, sed quia par negotiis neque supra erat.* Discretion is the great article; all those things are to be learned and only learned by keeping a great deal of the best company. Frequent those good houses where you have already a footing, and wriggle yourself somehow or other into every other. Haunt the courts particularly, in order to get that *routine. [June 20, 1751.]*

French and English Hunting. — Our abbé writes me word that you were gone to Compiègne; I am very glad of it; other courts must form you for your own. He tells me, too, that you have left off riding at the *manège;* I have no objection to that, it takes up a great deal of the morning; and if you have got a genteel and firm seat on horseback, it is enough for you, now that tilts and tournaments are laid aside. I suppose you have hunted at Compiègne. The king's hunting there, I am told, is a fine sight. The French manner of hunting is gentlemanlike; ours is only for bumpkins and boobies. The poor beasts here are pursued and run down by much greater beasts than themselves; and the true British fox-hunter is most undoubtedly a species appropriated and peculiar to this country, which no other part of the globe produces. *[June 30, 1751.]*

Polite Affection. — Remember to bring your mother some little presents; they need not be of value, but only marks of your affection and duty for one who has always been tenderly fond of you. You may bring Lady Chesterfield a little Martin snuff-box, of about five louis; and you need bring over no other presents; you and I not wanting *les petits présens pour entretenir l'amitié. [July 8, 1751.]*

Inattention. — Laziness of mind, or inattention, are as great enemies to knowledge, as incapacity; for, in truth, what difference is there between a man who will not, and a man who cannot, be informed? This difference only, that the former is justly to be blamed, and the latter to be pitied. And yet how many are there, very capable of receiving knowledge, who, from laziness, inattention, and incuriousness, will not so much as ask for it, much less take the least pains to acquire it.

Our young English travellers generally distinguish themselves by a voluntary privation of all that useful knowledge for which they are sent abroad; and yet, at that age, the most useful knowledge is the most easy to be acquired; conversation being the book, and the best book, in which it is contained. [*Jan. 2, 1752.*]

The Drama. — I could wish there were a treaty made between the French and the English theatres, in which both parties should make considerable concessions. The English ought to give up their notorious violations of all the unities; and all their massacres, racks, dead bodies, and mangled carcasses, which they so frequently exhibit upon their stage. The French should engage to have more action, and less declamation; and not to cram and crowd things together to almost a degree of impossibility, from a too scrupulous adherence to the unities. The English should restrain the licentiousness of their poets, and the French enlarge the liberty of theirs: their poets are the greatest slaves in their country, and that is a bold word; ours are the most tumultuous subjects in England, and that is saying a good deal. Under such regulations, one might hope to see a play, in which one should not be lulled to sleep by the length of a monotonical declamation, nor frightened and shocked by the barbarity of the action. The unity of time extended occasionally to three or four days, and the unity of place broke into, as far as the same street, or sometimes the same town; both which, I will affirm, are as probable, as four-and-twenty hours, and the same room.

More indulgence, too, in my mind, should be shown, than the French are willing to allow, to bright thoughts, and to shining images; for though I confess, it is not very natural for a hero or a princess to say fine things, in all the violence of grief, love, rage, etc., yet I can as well suppose that, as I can that they should talk to themselves for half an hour; which they must necessarily do, or no tragedy could be carried on, unless they had recourse to a much greater absurdity, the choruses of the ancients. Tragedy is of a nature, that one must see it with a degree of self-deception; we must lend ourselves, a little, to the delusion; and I am very willing to carry that complaisance a little further than the French do.

Tragedy must be something bigger than life, or it would not affect us. In nature the most violent passions are silent; in tragedy they must speak, and speak with dignity, too. Hence the necessity of their being written in verse, and, unfortunately for the French, from the weakness of their language, in rhymes. And for the same reason, Cato, the Stoic, expiring at Utica, rhymes masculine and feminine,52 at Paris; and fetches his last breath at London, in most harmonious and correct blank verse.

It is quite otherwise with comedy, which should be mere common life, and not one jot bigger. Every character should speak upon the stage, not only what it would utter in the situation there represented, but in the same manner in which it would express it. For which reason, I cannot allow rhymes in comedy, unless they were put into the mouth and came out of the mouth of a mad poet. But it is impossible to deceive one's self enough (nor is it the least necessary in comedy) to suppose a dull rogue of a usurer cheating, or *gros Jean* blundering, in the finest rhymes in the world.

As for operas, they are essentially too absurd and extravagant to mention: I look upon them as a magic scene, contrived to please the eyes and the ears, at the expense of the understanding; and I consider singing, rhyming, and chiming heroes, and princesses, and philosophers, as I do the hills, the trees, the birds, and the beasts, who amicably joined in one common country dance, to the irresistible tune of Orpheus's lyre. Whenever I go to an opera, I leave my sense and reason at the door with my half guinea, and deliver myself up to my eyes and my ears. [*Jan. 23, 1752.*]

Ridicule.—It is commonly said, and more particularly by Lord Shaftesbury, that ridicule is the best test of truth; for that it will not stick where it is not just. I deny it.53 A truth learned in a certain light, and attacked in certain words by men of wit and humor, may, and often doth, become ridiculous, at least so far, that the truth is only remembered and repeated for the sake of the ridicule. The overturn of Mary of Medicis into a river, where she was half drowned, would never have been remembered, if Madame de Vernueil, who saw it, had not said *la Reine boit.* Pleasure or malignity often gives ridicule a weight, which it does not deserve. [*Same date.*]

Comedies.—I chiefly mind dialogue and character in comedies. Let dull critics feed the carcasses of plays; give me the taste and the dressing. [*Feb. 6, 1752.*]

The Weight of Low People.—In courts a universal gentleness and *douceur dans les manières* is most absolutely necessary: an offended fool, or a slighted *valet de chambre*, may, very possibly, do more hurt at court, than ten men of merit can do you good. Fools, and low people, are always jealous of their dignity; and never forget nor forgive what they reckon a slight. [*Same date.*]

At Court.—There is a court garment, as well as a wedding garment, without which you will not be received. That garment is the *volto sciolto*: an imposing air, an elegant politeness, easy and engaging manners, universal attention, an insinuating gentleness, and all those *je ne sais quoi* that compose the *grâces*. [*Same date.*]

Perfection.—In all systems whatsoever, whether of religion, government, morals, etc., perfection is the object always proposed, though possibly unattainable; hitherto, at least, certainly unattained. However, those who aim carefully at the mark itself, will unquestionably come nearer to it than those who, from despair, negligence, or indolence, leave to chance the work of skill. This maxim holds equally true in common life; those who aim at perfection will come infinitely nearer it than those desponding or indolent spirits, who foolishly say to themselves, nobody is perfect; perfection is unattainable; to attempt it is chimerical; I shall do as well as others; why then should I give myself trouble to be what I never can, and what, according to the common course of things, I need not be, *perfect*? [*Feb. 20, 1752.*]

Omnis Homo.—I would have him have lustre as well as weight. Did you ever know anybody that reunited all these talents? Yes, I did; Lord Bolingbroke joined all the politeness, the manners, and the graces of a courtier, to the solidity of a statesman, and to the learning of a pedant. He was *omnis homo*; and pray what should hinder my boy of doing so too, if he hath, as I think he hath, all the other qualifications that you allow him? [*Same date.*]

Knowledge of Literature.—A gentleman should know those which I call classical works, in every language: such as Boileau, Corneille, Racine, Molière, etc., in French; Milton, Dryden, Pope, Swift, etc., in English; and the three authors above mentioned54 in Italian: whether you have any such in German I am not quite sure, nor, indeed, am I inquisitive. These sort of books adorn the mind, improve the fancy, are frequently alluded to by, and are often the subjects of conversations of, the best companies. As you have languages to read, and memory to retain them, the knowledge of them is very well worth the little pains it will cost you, and will enable you to shine in company. It is not pedantic to quote and allude to them, which it would be with regard to the ancients. [*March 2, 1752.*]

Nothing by Halves.—Whatever business you have, do it the first moment you can; never by halves, but finish it without interruption, if possible. Business must not be sauntered and trifled with; and you must not say to it, as Felix did to Paul, "at a more convenient season I will speak to thee." The most convenient season for business is the first; but study and business, in some measure, point out their own times to a man of sense;

time is much oftener squandered away in the wrong choice and improper methods of amusement and pleasures. [*March 5, 1752.*]

Formation of Manners.—Nothing forms a young man so much as being used to keep respectable and superior company, where a constant regard and attention is necessary. It is true, this is at first a disagreeable state of restraint; but it soon grows habitual, and consequently easy; and you are amply paid for it, by the improvement you make, and the credit it gives you. [*Same date.*]

The Best School.—Company, various company, is the only school for this knowledge. You ought to be, by this time, at least in the third form of that school, from whence the rise to the uppermost is easy and quick; but then you must have application and vivacity, you must not only bear with, but even seek, restraint in some companies, instead of stagnating in one or two only, where indolence and love of ease may be indulged. [*March 16, 1752.*]

Chesterfield's Prophecy.—I do not know what the Lord's anointed, His vicegerent upon earth, divinely appointed by Him, and accountable to none but Him for his actions, will either think or do, upon these symptoms of reason and good sense, which seem to be breaking out all over France; but this I foresee, that before the end of this century, the trade of both king and priest will not be half so good a one as it has been. Du Clos, in his reflections, hath observed, and very truly, *qu'il y a un germe de raison qui commence à se développer en France.* A *développement* that must prove fatal to regal and papal pretensions. Prudence may, in many cases, recommend an occasional submission to either; but when that ignorance, upon which an implicit faith in both could only be founded, is once removed, God's vicegerent, and Christ's vicar, will only be obeyed and believed, as far as what the one orders, and the other says, is conformable to reason and to truth. [*April 13, 1752.*]

Small Change.—In common life, one much oftener wants small money, and silver, than gold. Give me a man who has ready cash about him for present expenses, shillings, half-crowns, and crowns, which circulate easily; but a man who has only an ingot of gold about him is much above common purposes, and his riches are not handy nor convenient. Have as much gold as you please in one pocket, but take care always to keep change in the other; for you will much oftener have occasion for a shilling than for a guinea. [*Sept, 19, 1752.*]

Maxims.—My dear friend,—I never think my time so well employed, as when I think it employed to your advantage. In that view, I have thrown together, for your use, the enclosed maxims55 ; or, to speak more properly, observations of men and things; for I have no merit as to the invention; I am no system-monger; and, instead of giving way to my imagination, I have only consulted my memory; and my conclusions are all drawn from facts, not from fancy. Most maxim-mongers have preferred the prettiness to the justness of a thought, and the turn to the truth; but I have refused myself to everything that my own experience did not justify and confirm. [*Jan. 15, 1753.*]

A Wet Summer. — There never was so wet a summer as this has been, in the memory of man; we have not had one single day, since March, without some rain; but most days a great deal. I hope that does not affect your health, as great cold does; for, with all these inundations, it has not been cold. God bless you! [*Aug. 1, 1766.*]

The Last Greeting. — Poor Harte is in a miserable condition, is paralyzed in his left side, and can hardly speak intelligibly. I was with him yesterday. He inquired after you with great affection, and was in the utmost concern when I showed him your letter.

My own health is, as it has been ever since I was here last year. I am neither well nor ill, but *unwell*. I have, in a manner, lost the use of my legs; for though I can make a shift to crawl upon even ground for a quarter of an hour, I cannot go up or down stairs, unless supported by a servant.

God bless and grant you a speedy recovery! [*Oct. 17, 1768.*]

Here end the letters to Mr. Stanhope, as he died the 16th of November following.

To Mrs. Stanhope, then at Paris.

Madam: — A troublesome and painful inflammation in my eyes obliges me to use another hand than my own to acknowledge the receipt of your letter from Avignon, of the 27th past.

I am extremely surprised that Mrs. du Bouchet should have any objection to the manner in which your late husband desired to be buried, and which you, very properly, complied with. All I desire for my own burial is not to be buried alive; but how or where, I think, must be entirely indifferent to every rational creature.

I have no commission to trouble you with during your stay at Paris, from whence I wish you and the boys a good journey home, where I shall be very glad to see you all, and assure you of my being, with great truth, your faithful, humble servant, Chesterfield. [*March 16, 1769.*]

To the same, at London.

Madam: — The last time I had the pleasure of seeing you I was so taken up in playing with the boys that I forgot their more important affairs. How soon would you have them placed at school? When I know your pleasure as to that, I will send to Monsieur Perny to prepare everything for their reception. In the meantime, I beg that you will equip them thoroughly with clothes, linen, etc., all good, but plain, and give me the account, which I will pay, for I do not intend that from this time forward, the two boys should cost you one shilling. I am, with great truth, madam, your faithful, humble servant, Chesterfield. [*Wednesday.*]

Stanhope's Children. — Charles will be a scholar, if you please, but our little Philip, without being one, will be something or other as good, though I do not yet guess what. I am not of the opinion generally entertained in this country, that man lives by Greek and Latin alone; that is, by knowing a great many words of two dead languages, which nobody living knows perfectly, and which are of no use in the common intercourse of life. Useful knowledge, in my opinion, consists of modern languages, history, and geography; some Latin may be thrown into the bargain, in compliance with custom, and for closet amusement.

You are by this time certainly tired with this long letter, which I could prove to you from Horace's own words (for I am a *scholar*) to be a bad one; he says that water drinkers can write nothing good, so I am, with real truth and esteem, your most faithful, humble servant, Chesterfield. [*Nov. 4, 1770.*]

To Charles and Philip Stanhope.

The Last Letter. — I received, a few days ago, two, the best-written letters that I ever saw in my life: the one signed Charles Stanhope, the other Philip Stanhope. As for you, Charles, I do not wonder at it; for you will take pains, and are a lover of letters: but you idle rogue, you Phil, how came you to write so well, that one can almost say of you two, *et cantare pares et responderes parati*? Charles will explain this Latin to you.

I am told, Phil, that you have got a nickname at school, from your intimacy with Master *Strangeways*; and that they call you Master Strangerways; for, to be sure, you are a strange boy. Is this true?

Tell me what you would have me bring you both from hence, and I will bring it to you when I come to town. In the meantime, God bless you both! — Chesterfield. [Bath, Oct. 27, 1771.]

MAXIMS.56

A proper secrecy is the only mystery of able men; mystery is the only secrecy of weak and cunning ones.

A man who tells nothing, or who tells all, will equally have nothing told him.

If a fool knows a secret, he tells it because he is a fool; if a knave knows one, he tells it wherever it is his interest to tell it. But women and young men are very apt to tell what secrets they know, from the vanity of having been trusted. Trust none of these, whenever you can help it.

Inattention to the present business, be it what it will; the doing one thing, and thinking at the same time of another, or the attempting to do two things at once, are the never-failing signs of a little, frivolous mind.

A man who cannot command his temper, his attention, and his countenance, should not think of being a man of business. The weakest man in the world can avail himself of the passion of the wisest. The inattentive man cannot know the business, and consequently cannot do it. And he who cannot command his countenance, may e'en as well tell his thoughts as show them.

Distrust all those who love you extremely upon a very slight acquaintance, and without any visible reason. Be upon your guard, too, against those, who confess, as their weaknesses, all the cardinal virtues.

In your friendships, and in your enmities, let your confidence and your hostilities have certain bounds: make not the former dangerous, nor the latter irreconcilable. There are strange vicissitudes in business!

Smooth your way to the head, through the heart. The way of reason is a good one; but it is commonly something longer, and perhaps not so sure.

Spirit is now a very fashionable word: to act with spirit, to speak with spirit, means only, to act rashly, and to talk indiscreetly. An able man shows his spirit by gentle words and resolute actions: he is neither hot nor timid.

When a man of sense happens to be in that disagreeable situation, in which he is obliged to ask himself more than once, *What shall I do?* he will answer himself, Nothing. When his reason points out to him no good way, or at least no one way less bad than another, he will stop short, and wait for light. A little busy mind runs on at all events, must be doing; and, like a blind horse, fears no dangers because he sees none. *Il faut savoir s'ennuyer.*

Patience is a most necessary qualification for business; many a man would rather you heard his story than granted his request. One must seem to hear the unreasonable demands of the petulant, unmoved, and the tedious details of the dull, untired. That is the least price a man must pay for a high station.

It is always right to detect a fraud, and to perceive a folly; but it is often very wrong to expose either. A man of business should always have his eyes open; but must often seem to have them shut.

In courts, nobody should be below your management and attention: the links that form the court-chain are innumerable and inconceivable. You must hear with patience the dull grievances of a gentleman usher, or a page of the back-stairs; who, very probably, lies with some near relation of the favorite maid, of the favorite mistress, of the favorite minister, or perhaps of the king himself; and who, consequently, may do you more dark or indirect good, or harm, than the first man of quality.

One good patron at court may be sufficient, provided you have no personal enemies; and, in order to have none, you must sacrifice (as the Indians do to the Devil) most of your passions, and much of your time, to the numberless evil beings that infest it; in order to prevent and avert the mischiefs they can do you.

A young man, be his merit what it will, can never raise himself; but must, like the ivy round the oak, twine himself round some man of great power and interest. You must belong to a minister some time, before anybody will belong to you. And an inviolable fidelity to that minister, even in his disgrace, will be meritorious, and recommend you to the next. Ministers love a personal, much more than a party attachment.

As kings are begotten and born like other men, it is to be presumed that they are of the human species; and perhaps, had they the same education, they might prove like other men. But, flattered from their cradles, their hearts are corrupted, and their heads are turned, so that they seem to be a species by themselves. No king ever said to himself: *Homo sum, nihil humani a me alienum puto.*

Flattery cannot be too strong for them; drunk with it from their infancy, like old drinkers, they require drams.

They prefer a personal attachment to a public service, and reward it better. They are vain and weak enough to look upon it as a free-will offering to their merit, and not as a burnt sacrifice to their power.

If you would be a favorite of your king, address yourself to his weaknesses. An application to his reason will seldom prove very successful.

In courts, bashfulness and timidity are as prejudicial on one hand, as impudence and rashness are on the other. A steady assurance, and a cool intrepidity, with an exterior modesty, are the true and necessary medium.

Never apply for what you see very little probability of obtaining; for you will, by asking improper and unattainable things, accustom the ministers to refuse you so often, that they will find it easy to refuse you the properest and most reasonable ones. It is a common but a most mistaken rule at court, to ask for everything, in order to get something: you do get something by it, it is true; but that something is refusals and ridicule.

There is a court jargon, a chit-chat, a small talk, which turns singly upon trifles; and which, in a great many words, says little or nothing. It stands fools instead of what they cannot say, and men of sense instead of what they should not say. It is the proper language of levees, drawing-rooms, and ante-chambers; it is necessary to know it.

Whatever a man is at court, he must be genteel and well-bred; that cloak covers as many follies, as that of charity does sins. I knew a man of great quality, and in a great station at court, considered and respected, whose highest character was, that he was humbly proud, and genteelly dull.

It is hard to say which is the greatest fool; he who tells the whole truth, or he who tells no truth at all. Character is as necessary in business as in trade. No man can deceive often in either.

At court, people embrace without acquaintance, serve one another without friendship, and injure one another without hatred. Interest, not sentiment, is the growth of that soil.

A difference of opinion, though in the merest trifles, alienates little minds, especially of high rank. It is full as easy to commend as to blame a great man's cook, or his tailor; it is shorter, too; and the objects are no more worth disputing about, than the people are worth disputing with. It is impossible to inform, but very easy to displease them.

A cheerful, easy countenance and behavior are very useful at court; they make fools think you are a good-natured man; and they make designing men think you are an undesigning one.

There are some occasions in which a man must tell half his secret, in order to conceal the rest; but there is seldom one in which a man should tell it all. Great skill is necessary to know how far to go, and where to stop.

Ceremony is necessary in courts, as the outwork and defence of manners.

Flattery, though a base coin, is the necessary pocket-money at court; where, by custom and consent, it has obtained such a currency, that it is no longer a fraudulent, but a legal payment.

If a minister refuses you a reasonable request, and either slights or injures you, if you have not the power to gratify your resentment, have the wisdom to conceal and dissemble it. Seeming good humor on your part may prevent rancor on his, and perhaps bring things aright again: but if you have the power to hurt, hint modestly that, if provoked, you may possibly have the will too. Fear, when real, and well founded, is perhaps a more prevailing motive at courts than love.

At court, many more people can hurt, than can help you; please the former, but engage the latter.

Awkwardness is a more real disadvantage than it is generally thought to be; it often occasions ridicule, it always lessens dignity.

A man's own good breeding is his best security against other people's ill-manners.

Good breeding carries along with it a dignity, that is respected by the most petulant. Ill breeding invites and authorizes the familiarity of the most timid. No man ever said a pert thing to the Duke of Marlborough. No man ever said a civil one (though many a flattering one) to Sir Robert Walpole.

When the old clipped money was called in for a new coinage in King William's time, to prevent the like for the future, they stamped on the edges of the crown pieces these words, *et decus et tutamen*. That is exactly the case of good breeding.

Knowledge may give weight, but accomplishments only give lustre; and many more people see than weigh.

Most arts require long study and application; but the most useful art of all, that of pleasing, requires only the desire.

It is to be presumed that a man of common-sense, who does not desire to please, desires nothing at all, since he must know that he cannot obtain anything without it.

A skilful negotiator will most carefully distinguish between the little and the great objects of his business, and will be as frank and open in the former as he will be secret and pertinacious in the latter.

He will, by his manners and address, endeavor, at least, to make his public adversaries his personal friends. He will flatter and engage the man, while he counterworks the minister; and he will never alienate people's minds from him, by wrangling for points, either absolutely unattainable, or not worth attaining. He will make even a merit of giving up what he could not or would not carry, and sell a trifle for a thousand times its value.

A foreign minister, who is concerned in great affairs, must necessarily have spies in his pay; but he must not too easily credit their informations, which are never exactly true, often very false. His best spies will always be those whom he does not pay, but whom he has engaged in his service by his dexterity and address, and who think themselves nothing less than spies.

There is a certain jargon which in French I should call *un persiflage d'affaires*, that a foreign minister ought to be perfectly master of, and may use very advantageously at great entertainments in mixed companies, and in all occasions where he must speak and should say nothing. Well turned and well spoken, it seems to mean something, though in truth it means nothing. It is a kind of political *badinage*, which prevents or removes a thousand difficulties to which a foreign minister is exposed in mixed conversations.

If ever the *volto sciolto* and the *pensieri stretti* are necessary, they are so in these affairs. A grave, dark, reserved, and mysterious air has *fœnum in cornu*. An even, easy, unembarrassed one invites confidence, and leaves no room for guesses and conjectures.

Both stimulation and dissimulation are absolutely necessary for a foreign minister; and yet they must stop short of falsehood and perfidy: that middle point is the difficult one: there ability consists. He must often seem pleased, when he is vexed; and grave, when he is pleased; but he must never say either: that would be falsehood — an indelible stain to character.

A foreign minister should be a most exact economist. An expense proportioned to his appointments and fortune is necessary; but, on the other hand, debt is inevitable ruin to him. It sinks him into disgrace at the court where he resides, and into the most servile and abject dependence on the court that sent him. As he cannot resent ill usage, he is sure to have enough of it.

The Duc de Sully observes very justly, in his Memoirs, that nothing contributed more to his rise, than that prudent economy which he had observed from his youth, and by which he had always a sum of money beforehand, in case of emergencies.

It is very difficult to fix the particular point of economy; the best error of the two is on the parsimonious side. That may be corrected; the other cannot.

The reputation of generosity is to be purchased pretty cheap; it does not depend so much upon a man's general expense, as it does upon his giving handsomely where it is proper to give at all. A man, for instance, who should give a servant four shillings would pass for covetous, while he who gave him a crown would be reckoned generous; so that the difference of those two opposite characters turns upon one shilling. A man's character, in that particular, depends a great deal upon the report of his own servants; a mere trifle above common wages makes their report favorable.

Take care always to form your establishment so much within your income as to leave a sufficient fund for unexpected contingencies and a prudent liberality. There is hardly a year, in any man's life, in which a small sum of ready money may not be employed to great advantage.

POLITICAL MAXIMS FROM CARDINAL DE RETZ.57

It is often madness to engage in a conspiracy; but nothing is so effectual to bring people afterward to their senses, at least for a time. As in such undertakings, the danger subsists, even after the business is over; this obliges to be prudent and circumspect in the succeeding moments.

2. A middling understanding, being susceptible of unjust suspicions, is consequently, of all characters, the least fit to head a faction; as the most indispensable qualification in such a chief is to suppress, in many occasions, and to conceal in all, even the best grounded suspicions.

3. Nothing animates and gives strength to a commotion so much as the ridicule of him against whom it is raised.

4. Among people used to affairs of moment, secrecy is much less uncommon than is generally believed.

5. Descending to the little is the surest way of attaining to an equality with the great.

6. Fashion, though powerful in all things, is not more so in any, than in being well or ill at court. There are times when disgrace is a kind of fire, that purifies all bad qualities, and illuminates every good one. There are others, in which the being out of favor is unbecoming a man of character.

7. Sufferings, in people of the first rank, supply the want of virtue.

8. There is a confused kind of jumble, which practice sometimes teaches; but it is never to be understood by speculation.

9. The greatest powers cannot injure a man's character, whose reputation is unblemished among his party.

10. We are as often duped by diffidence, as by confidence.

11. The greatest evils are not arrived at their utmost period until those who are in power have lost all sense of shame. At such a time those who should obey shake off all respect and subordination. Then is lethargic indolence roused; but roused by convulsions.

12. A veil ought always to be drawn over whatever may be said or thought concerning the rights of the people, or of kings; which agree best when least mentioned.58

13. There are, at times, situations so very unfortunate, that whatever is undertaken must be wrong. Chance, alone, never throws people into such dilemmas; and they happen only to those who bring them upon themselves.

14. It is more unbecoming a minister to say, than to do, silly things.

15. The advice given to a minister, by an obnoxious person, is always thought bad.

16. It is as dangerous, and almost as criminal, with princes, to have the power of doing good, as the will of doing evil.

17. Timorous minds are much more inclined to deliberate than to resolve.

18. It appears ridiculous to assert, but it is not the less true, that at Paris, during the popular commotions, the most violent will not quit their homes past a stated hour.

19. Flexibility is the most requisite qualification for the management of great affairs.

20. It is more difficult for the member of a faction to live with those of his own party, than to act against those who oppose it.

21. The greatest dangers have their allurements, if the want of success is likely to be attended with a degree of glory. Middling dangers are horrid, when the loss of reputation is the inevitable consequence of ill success.

22. Violent measures are always dangerous, but when necessary, may then be looked upon as wise. They have, however, the advantage of never being matter of indifferency; and, when well concerted, must be decisive.

23. There may be circumstances, in which even prudence directs us to trust entirely to chance.

24. Everything in this world has its critical moment, and the height of good conduct consists in knowing and seizing it.

25. Profligacy, joined to ridicule, forms the most abominable and most dangerous of all characters.

26. Weak minds never yield when they ought.

27. Variety of sights have the greatest effect upon the mob, and also upon numerous assemblies, who, in many respects, resemble mobs.

28. Examples taken from past times have infinitely more power over the minds of men, than any of the age in which they live. Whatever we see,

grows familiar; and perhaps the consulship of Caligula's horse might not have astonished us so much as we are apt to imagine.

29. Weak minds are commonly overpowered by clamor.

30. We ought never to contend for what we are not likely to obtain.

31. The instant in which we receive the most favorable accounts, is just that wherein we ought to redouble our vigilance, even in regard to the most trifling circumstances.

32. It is dangerous to have a known influence over people; as thereby we become responsible even for what is done against our will.

33. One of the greatest difficulties in civil war is, that more art is required to know what should be concealed from our friends, than what ought to be done against our enemies.

34. Nothing lowers a great man so much, as not seizing the decisive moment of raising his reputation. This is seldom neglected, but with a view to fortune; by which mistake, it is not unusual to miss both.

35. The possibility of remedying imprudent actions is commonly an inducement to commit them.

36. Every numerous assembly is a mob; consequently everything there depends upon instantaneous turns.

37. Whatever measure seems hazardous, and is in reality not so, is generally a wise one.

38. Irresolute minds always adopt with facility whatever measure can admit of different issues, and consequently do not require an absolute decision.

39. In momentous affairs, no step is indifferent.

40. There are times in which certain people are always in the right.

41. Nothing convinces persons of a weak understanding so effectually as what they do not comprehend.

42. When factions are only upon the defensive, they ought never to do that which may be delayed. Upon such occasions, nothing is so troublesome as the restlessness of subalterns; who think a state of inaction total destruction.

43. Those who head factions have no way of maintaining their authority, but by preventing or quieting discontent.

44. A certain degree of fear produces the same effects as rashness.

45. In affairs of importance, the choice of words is of as much consequence, as it would be superfluous in those of little moment.

46. During those calms which immediately succeed violent storms, nothing is more difficult for ministers than to act properly; because, while flattery increases, suspicions are not yet subsided.

47. The faults of our friends ought never to anger us so far as to give an advantage to our enemies.

48. The talent of insinuation is more useful than that of persuasion, as everybody is open to insinuation, but scarce any to persuasion.

49. In matters of a delicate nature, all unnecessary alterations are dangerous, because odious.

50. The best way to compel weak-minded people to adopt our opinion, is to frighten them from all others, by magnifying their danger.

51. We must run all hazards, where we think ourselves in a situation to reap some advantage, even from the want of success.

52. Irresolute men are diffident in resolving upon the means, even when they are determined upon the end.

53. It is almost a sure game, with crafty men, to make them believe we intend to deceive those whom we mean to serve.

54. One of the greatest difficulties with princes is in the being often obliged, in order to serve them, to give advice, the true reasons of which we dare not mention.

55. The saying things which we foresee will not be pleasing, can only be softened by the greatest appearance of sincerity.

56. We ought never to trifle with favor. If real, we should hastily seize the advantage; if pretended, avoid the allurement.

57. It is very inconsequent to enter into engagements upon suppositions we think impossible, and yet it is very usual.

58. The generality of mankind pay less attention to arguments urged against their opinion, than to such as may engage the disputant to adopt their own.

59. In times of faction and intrigue, whatever appears inert is reckoned mysterious by those who are not accustomed to affairs of moment.

60. It is never allowable in an inferior to equal himself in words to a superior, although he may rival him in actions.

61. Every man whom chance alone has, by some accident, made a public character, hardly ever fails of becoming, in a short time, a ridiculous private one.

62. The greatest imperfection of men is the complacency with which they are willing to think others not free from faults, of which they are themselves conscious.

63. Experience only can teach men not to prefer what strikes them for the present moment, to what will have much greater weight with them hereafter.

64. In the management of important business, all turn to raillery must be more carefully avoided than in any other.

65. In momentous transactions, words cannot be sufficiently weighed.

66. The permanency of most friendships depends upon the continuity of good fortune.

67. Whoever assembles the multitude will raise commotions.

LORD CHESTERFIELD'S REMARKS UPON THE FOREGOING MAXIMS.

I have taken the trouble of extracting and collecting, for your use, the foregoing Political Maxims of the Cardinal de Retz, in his Memoirs. They are not aphorisms of his invention, but the true and just observations of his own experience, in the course of great business. My own experience attests the truth of them all. Read them over with attention as here above, and then read with the same attention, and *tout de suite*, the Memoirs, where you will find the facts and characters from whence those observations are drawn, or to which they are applied; and they will reciprocally help to fix each other in your mind. I hardly know any book so necessary for a young man to read and remember. You will there find how great business is really carried on; very differently from what people, who have never been concerned in it, imagine. You will there see what courts and courtiers really are, and observe that they are neither so good as they should be, nor so bad as they are thought by most people. The court poet, and the sullen, cloistered pedant, are equally mistaken in their notions, or at least in the accounts they give us of them. You will observe the coolness in general, the perfidy in some cases, and the truth in a very few, of court friendships. This will teach you the prudence of a general distrust, and the imprudence of making no exception to that rule, upon good and tried grounds. You will see the utility of good breeding toward one's greatest enemies, and the high imprudence and folly of either insulting or injurious expressions.

FOOTNOTES

1 The greatest English writer of the present day thus sums up the eighteenth century: — "An age of which Hoadly was the bishop, and Walpole the minister, and Pope the poet, and Chesterfield the wit, and Tillotson the ruling doctor." — Newman, *Essays Critical and Historical*, i. 388.

2 For another, very different, view of the life and studies at Cambridge at the time, see the *Life of Ambrose Bonwicke* (1694-1714).

3 ["*Pasquin.* A Dramatic Satire on the Times, by Henry Fielding. Acted at the Haymarket, 1736; 1740." (Baker.)]

4 ["*King Charles I.* Hist Tr. by W. Havard, 1737." (Ibid.).]

5 Chesterfield says he had been accustomed to read and translate the great masterpieces to improve and form his style. His indebtedness to Milton in his *Areopagitica* in the above passage is obvious.

6 See Letter CCXV., also CCXII.

7 It is just possible, though I have nowhere seen it affirmed, that Voltaire and Chesterfield may have met, still earlier, in Holland. For in 1713 they were both there. Their attainments there were all but parallel, Voltaire succumbing to a fatal passion in 1713, which did not, to our knowledge, overtake Chesterfield till his second visit in 1729.

8 He must just have escaped traveling from Leipzig to Berlin with Lessing. Both took the journey in February, 1749.

9 For his fine sense of the quality of words witness: "An unharmonious and rugged period at this time shocks my ears, and I, like all the rest of the world, will willingly exchange and give up some degree of rough sense for a good degree of pleasing sound."

10 Characteristically, no mention is made of Shaftesbury nor of Hutcheson.

11 *Cf.* Sir Walter Raleigh's "Every Man's Folly ought to be his greatest secret." — (*Instructions to his Son.*)

12 "A wise Atheist (if such a thing there is) would, for his own interest and character in the world, pretend to some religion." — Letter CLXXX.

13 In this Essay, by the late M. Sainte-Beuve, nothing has been altered, although, in one or two places, even his critical acuteness seems to have missed its point.

14 This is no longer a conjecture, but a certainty, after what I read in the edition of *Lord Chesterfield's Letters*, published in London by Lord Mahon in 1847 (4 vols.). See vol. iii., page 159. I was not acquainted with this edition when I wrote my article. — C. de S. B.

15 This was written in June, 1850.

16 This first letter will form a key to Chesterfield's character. It is partly badinage, and yet contains the elements of his lordship's idea. He has already begun to teach "Mr. Stanhope," and addresses as Monsieur a child of the mature age of five years. We have purposely omitted other letters, some in Latin, *Phillipo Stanhope, adhuc puerulo*, which contain merely historical and geographical information fit for a little schoolboy.

17 Lord Chesterfield was, as will be afterwards seen, particularly anxious that his son should imbibe political, geographical, and historical knowledge, hence these details to a child of five.

18 Young Mr. Stanhope's tutor.

19 In a previous letter, which has been lost, Chesterfield has been teaching rhetoric to a boy of about seven years old, for, referring to it, he says: "En vérité je crois que vous êtes le premier garcon à qui, *avant l'âge de huit ans*, on ait jamais parlé des figures de la rhétorique, comme j'ai fait dans ma dernière."

20 We learn by a subsequent reference that the little fellow wished not to be called Colas, but Polyglot, from knowing already three or four languages.

21 Careful Imitation. — *Philip Chesterfield to his dear little boy Philip Stanhope, wishing health, etc.* Your last letter was very grateful to me; not only was it nicely written, but in it you promise to take great care and to win,

deservedly, true praise. But I must say plainly that I much suspect you of having had the help of a good and able master in composing it; and he being your guide and adviser, it will be your own fault if you do not acquire elegancy of style, learning, and all that can make you good and wise. I entreat you, therefore, carefully to imitate so good a pattern; the more you regard him the more you will love me. [*About July, 1741.*]

22 In the beginning of this letter, which contains a lesson upon Julius Cæsar, Chesterfield says: "You know so much more and learn so much better than any boy of your age, that you see I do not treat you like a boy, but write to you on subjects fit for men to consider."

23 So also Home,—

"Amen! and virtue is its own reward."

Douglas, Act. iii. Sc. 1.

And Claudian, quoted by Chesterfield,

"Ipsa quidem virtus pretium sibi, solaque latè

Fortunæ secura nitet," etc.

24 Written in Latin. *Philippus Chesterfield, Phillippo Stanhope adhuc puerulo, sed eras e pueritiâ egressuro. S. D.* Dated, Kalend, Maii, 1741.

25 In the compilation called "Lord Chesterfield's Maxims," wherein part of this letter is given, all the characteristic points are left out. Thus, where Chesterfield reminds his son that manner is of consequence in pleasing, *especially the women*, the purist has excised the words in italics.

26 His Lordship's badinage, or it may be sarcasm, which the little boy quickly perceived.

27 His lordship was then Viceroy of Ireland.

28 Mr. Stanhope was then travelling with his tutor in Germany.

29 A good natured but somewhat silly book in which M. L'Abbé instructs certain young ladies and gentlemen by means of sundry conversations and reflections.

30 His lordship had during this year been made one of his Majesty's Secretaries of State.

31 Chesterfield had inclosed in a letter from Mr. Stanhope's mamma one from his own sister, thanking the boy for some Arquebusade water. His lordship sent a rough copy of a polite answer to this note.

32 Lord Chesterfield had been urging his son to send a Dresden tea-service to his mother, which he did.

33 A pun; the pillars from Canons in Middlesex.

34 It is well, in the present state of society, to reflect upon the intimacy here shown between persons in trade and those in high life.

35 A somewhat curious use of the phrase, but well explained by Johnson.

36 De Retz, from whose "Mémoires" Lord Chesterfield quoted a sentence in the commencement of the letter.

37 The author, as he says, often repeats himself; see *ante*.

38 Pic-nic. Johnson does not mention this word, nor do his predecessors, Ashe and Bailey. Richardson does not give it even in his supplement. Worcester cites Widegren, 1788; this then is the earliest use of the word by an author of weight.

39 On a German question.

40 An open face with a close (or secret) mind.

41 This little note is inserted to show that Lord Chesterfield's repetitions were not unknown to himself. The most flagrant we have omitted.

42 As indeed did George III. *teste* the anecdote of Kemble: "Mr. Kemble, *obleige* me with a pinch of snuff." "It would become your Majesty's royal mouth better to say *oblige*."

43 We retain this as a picture of the morals of the time, and to satisfy the reader's curiosity as to the subject of so much care on the part of his father.

44 "Letters on the Spirit of Patriotism, on the Idea of a Patriot King."

45 A notorious, wretched debauchee, who has been pilloried into a miserable and degraded immortality by Arbuthnot, Pope and Hogarth; the painter has given us his portrait in "The Harlot's Progress," plate 1. Pope has set him up as an instance of that hardest trial to good men, the success of the wicked:

"Should some lone temple, nodding to its fall,

For Chartres' head reserve the nodding wall."

And Arbuthnot wrote the most tremendously severe epitaph in the whole range of literature on him while yet alive: "Here *continueth to rot* the body of Colonel Francis Chartres," etc. Finally, Chesterfield points him out to his son as the most notorious blasted rascal in the world — blasted, indeed, as by lightning. It is needless to say that this word is not used as a vulgar oath, but to point out a man whose name is, as the Bible of 1551 has it: "Marred forever by *blastynge*."

46 Benedict XIV. — the amiable Lambertini, who was thought by Chesterfield too much of a savant and a man of the world to be foolishly devout.

47 The lady was turned fifty, and Chesterfield recommends her as a chaperone.

48 Strong as this reprobation is, it is as much needed to-day as when written; the whole English race (if we credit *Westminster Review*, March, 1869), especially the upper class, is suffering from the awful effects of vice.

49 Thus Englished by the famous Tom Brown:

"I do not love thee, Dr. Fell, the reason why I cannot tell,

But this I know and know full well, I do *not* love thee, Dr. Fell."

50 The Maréchal de Richelieu.

51 This single word implies decorum, good breeding, and propriety.

52 As to terminations, so careful were the best French poets of their rhymes.

53 Chesterfield had at once perceived the emptiness of the saying, which is certainly not in *ipsissimis verbis* of Lord Shaftesbury. "We have," says Carlyle, in his "Essay on Voltaire," "oftener than once endeavored to attach some meaning to that aphorism, vulgarly imputed to Shaftesbury — which, however, *we can find nowhere in his works*, — that ridicule is the test of truth." In the "Characteristics of Enthusiasm," sec. 2, there is this sentence, which comes very near it: — "How is it, etc., that we (Christians) appear such cowards in reasoning, and are so afraid *to stand the test of ridicule*"; but further on (ed. 1733, vol. i.) he asks: "For what ridicule can lie against reason? or how can any one of the least justice of thought admire a ridicule

wrong placed? Nothing is more ridiculous than this itself." Shaftesbury often returns to this subject; see "Errors in Wit," etc.

54 Ariosto, Tasso, and Boccaccio: the Orlando, Gierusalemme, and Decamerone.

55 See "Maxims,".

56 These maxims are referred to on page 324.

57 Upon the back of the original is written, in Mr. Stanhope's hand, "Excellent Maxims, but more calculated for the meridian of France or Spain than of England."

58 This Maxim, as well as several others, evidently prove they were written by a man subject to despotic government.